TWO SERMONS PREACHED TO TH...

SERMONS BY F.E. P...

COMMENTARY BY E. RAYMOND CAP...

the USA
in
Bible
Prophecy

REVISED & EXPANDED

The U.S.A. in Bible Prophecy

Our Great Country Foretold
In The Holy Scriptures
and
The Battle of Armageddon

*Two discourses delivered
in the Capitol of the United States,
at the request of several Members of Congress,
on the anniversary of Washington's birthday, 1857.*

by
F. E. Pitts
of Nashville, Tennessee

with
added Commentary by
E. Raymond Capt

also
George Washington's Vision
John Grady, M.D.

NEWLY REVISED AND EXPANDED EDITION

ISBN 0-934666-49-0

"Thou hast magnified thy word above all thy name."
PSALM cxxxviii, 2

Doomed by an edict written in the sky,

The monarchies of earth shall be no more:

Heaven's sealed wonders open to the eye

In rising glories on the western shore.

Foreword

Many Christians today have not been exposed to what our forefathers believed and understood. Whether through God's purposeful blindness or due to modern-day revisionists' intense desire to rewrite our Christian American history, the fact remains, we have lost our true identity, our heritage, our Israel roots. Nevertheless, the prophetic Scriptures clearly speak of an immense land reserved for regathered Israel in the latter days. This book will offer proof that the United States of America possesses all of the identifying marks of that land. Sermons and documents by the Founding Fathers testify to their belief that they were the Israel people of the latter days, and that the Old Testament prophecies were being fulfilled in their undertakings. It would be wise for us who are living in these last days to look again, closer, at the past generations of our great nation to relearn what they knew about America's critical role in Bible prophecy.

The USA in Bible Prophecy begins with a powerful sermon by Rev. F. E. Pitts of Nashville, Tennessee, before a joint session of Congress (1857), in which he presents compelling evidence that the United States is the providential "great Israel nation" to arise in the latter days, the nation "born at once" (Isa. 66:8) - July 4, 1776, possessing the "only true religion (Christianity), and a divinely sanctioned form of civil government." He believed our American-Israel people were ordained by God with a divine mission to be "a city set on a hill" (witness of Christ to the world).

E. Raymond Capt (1914-2008), noted author, archaeologist, and historian, agreed with Rev. Pitts and devoted almost sixty years of his life tracing the history of the Israel people from biblical times to the present day. He wrote numerous books showing that the Anglo-Saxon-Celtic and kindred peoples of Western Europe and America descended from the tribes of ancient Israel. Excerpts from *Our Great Seal* and *Abrahamic Covenant* are included in this book to offer additional light on this important subject.

Finally, because our nation is experiencing unprecedented turbulent events that seem to increase in intensity and frequency (Scripture compares this time to the pangs of childbirth.), many Christians sense the approaching prophesied end of this age before the return of Christ. Therefore a second timely sermon by Rev. Pitts has been added to this revised addition, entitled **"Battle of Armageddon."** Living as he did, 80 years after we became a nation and at a time when Russia was a friend to America, he revealed through a keen insight into biblical prophecy the rise of Russia as a world power and her future war with America and Christianity. Speaking of this last great conflict, he stated: "We look to the future for the finale of these startling wonders, to be fulfilled in a conflict that will enlist all nations, stir the world with commotion, and drench the earth with blood."

George Washington had a vision of the same final battle with multitudes from many nations coming against the United States, culminating in deliverance by the hand of Almighty God. His vision at Valley Forge, also recorded in the Congressional Record, offers a second witness to this predicted event.

The words of this book offer hope and truth that the plan of God, as set forth from the foundation of the world, is moving forward to usher in the **Kingdom of God** on earth. Christian Israel-America, then, has a sobering responsibility at the end of this age as His "light bearing" servant people!

Table of Contents

Our pilgrim fathers called themselves the "Seed of Abraham," "God's Servants," "Children of Jacob," "His Chosen." They built our nation upon the Laws of God and the teachings of Christ, and the United States of America became the greatest nation in history.

Please consider . . .

Standing on the western shores of Europe 500 years ago, you could not see nor visualize a great continent that lay to the west; only what seemed to be an endless stretch of the Atlantic Ocean. Yet there was a great continent out there to the west.

Now may I ask you, "Did Jesus Christ know of this North American Continent?"
Your only answer could be, *"Yes, of course He did."*

Let me ask another question, "Did Jesus Christ know that a great nation would be established here?" *"Of course He did!"*

Still another question please – "Did Jesus Christ know this great nation (yet to be born) would be Christian from its beginning?"
"Of course He knew that, for He Himself is the source and Author of the faith we call 'Christian.'"

Now one more question, "Is it possible that this great nation, known to Jesus Christ, was never mentioned, indicated, or foretold in the Bible?"

Consider these, *"I will make of thee a great nation"* (Genesis 12:2). *"The kingdom of God shall be given to a nation bringing forth the fruits thereof"* (Matthew 21:43). Where is this great nation? Where is that nation which is bringing forth the fruits of the Kingdom? The answer is quite obvious: you are living in it. See to it that you make your calling and election sure.

– W. B. Record

*"Man will occasionally stumble over the truth,
but most of the time
he will pick himself up and continue."*
– Winston Churchill

THE
UNITED STATES OF AMERICA
Foretold in the Holy Scriptures

One of two discourses delivered
in the Capitol of the United States,
at the request of several Members of Congress,
on the anniversary of Washington's birthday, 1857.

Rev. F. E. Pitts

IN entering the sublime arcana of inspired prophecy, we are deeply impressed with a scene that is laid in the land of Midian, where, from the burning bush, the voice of Almighty God arrested the attention of the wondering prophet: *"Put off thy shoes from off thy feet: for the place whereon thou standest is holy ground."*

No subject presented to the human mind imposes profounder reverence, greater caution, and deeper research than an elucidation of prophetic truth; and yet no theme has been more prolific of fanaticism among the incautious and adventurous in almost every age.

We must look to the Scriptures themselves for direction to a true and legitimate interpretation of their own meaning. It is important also to discriminate between "secret things that belong to God, and things that are revealed, which belong to us and our children." For want of this discernment, Millerism, and all that class of fanatical fancies, have deluded misguided thousands. Whenever, therefore, an interpreter of prophecy attempts to tell when the day of judgment will come, just rest assured he is wise above what is written; for we are taught by the Great Prophet Himself, *"Of that day, and hour, knoweth no man; no, not the angels of heaven, but my Father only."* This Divine announcement should always quiet such unauthorized pretensions.

It must be universally conceded that the Almighty has interdicted a knowledge of some sublime subjects, which He alone will fully reveal and explain by their own accomplishment. Notwithstanding, it is equally evident that there are certain portions of prophetic truth that He Himself designed should be understood by the sons of men, for it is written, *"Blessed is he that readeth and they that hear the words of this prophecy."* Here, then, is a Divine encouragement to study inspired prophecy. But how can we be beneficiaries of this promise, though we may both read and hear, if, at the same time, we cannot understand them?

A few self-evident propositions we will now submit as indispensable principles for the investigation of prophecy – principles that must form the only true and infallible criteria to determine their intended meaning.

First. All prophecy is either plain and literal, or obscure and symbolical.

Second. A plain and literal prophecy may be understood prior to fulfillment, just as well as subsequent to the event predicted. For example, Jesus Christ said, *"There shall not be left here one stone upon another that shall not be thrown down."* His meaning was too obvious to be misunderstood.

Third. But an obscure or symbolic prophecy cannot possibly be fully known, however impressive the general outline of the subject; yet the special application of the prediction to time, event, and circumstances cannot be understood until fulfillment settles the true meaning. There may be several interpretations of an obscure prophecy offered a priori, provided they are legitimate; that is, if such definitions are not unreasonable or incompatible with the nature of the subject. Nevertheless, we must bide our time till fulfillment determines the meaning intended. As an example, it is written, *"Behold, I will send you Elijah the prophet before the coming of the great and dreadful day of the Lord."* Now, it is evident that one legitimate interpretation of this prophecy was the same entertained by the Jews, that God would send the old prophet in person, for it expressly states, *"Elijah the prophet."* But it so happened that another man altogether, John the Baptist, coming *"in the spirit and power of Elias,"* is said by Christ to be *"the Elias which was for to come."*

Fourth. A perfect coincidence of character, circumstances, and events with any given prophecy, is perfect fulfillment. This is so plain and patent that we cannot deny it without denying the very proof of the Messiahship of the Son of God. When John sent his disciples to Christ to inquire, *"Art thou he that should come, or do we look for another?"* *"Jesus answered and said unto them, Go and show John again those things which ye do hear and see: the blind receive their sight, and the lame walk, and the lepers are cleansed, and the deaf hear, the dead are raised up, and the poor have the gospel preached unto them."* As much as if he had said, John will have sense enough to know that in whomsoever these coincidences are found, he is the Messiah.

With these principles to guide us, we proceed to the investigation of our subject.

The United States of America, our great country, is foretold in the Holy Scriptures.

We are fully apprised that the novelty and sublimity of our subject, upon its bare announcement, will awaken the incredulity of some, and enlist the opposition of others.

To all such we politely bespeak the courtesy of a candid hearing. We are not concerned that you receive or reject the truth of this theory, but we **are concerned** that you carefully examine the testimony upon which it rests. Do you believe the Holy Scriptures? "Then hear me for my cause."

But that you may understand that we do not attempt to prove what is unreasonable and absurd, we propose the following question:

Is it at all probable that our great country, with its teeming magnificence, now the fear and glory of all lands, **would have been overlooked by prophecy?** How comes it to pass that smaller countries, and lesser kingdoms, retired hamlets, solitary island, and seaport towns; that Edom, Moab, Egypt, and Syria; that Tarshish, Tyre, and Sidon, with the rest, are particularly programmed upon the inspired page, and *our* land is the only portion of God's terra-firma that is proscribed a place in *the book* – that *prophetic book* that professes to map the world till the end of time? Has the inspired penman no account, no place for a nation that is at this very moment telling more upon the intellectual and moral destiny of the world than any other under heaven? Do you believe it? And yet you must believe it if our theory is a fable.

The possibility of the *truthfulness* of our subject is certainly deeply interesting; the probability of the **fact** is startling; but the clear and unanswerable demonstration of that truth is actually sublime.

The predictions of the Bible touching the nations, down to the destruction of the Jewish capitol, are indeed but a literal history of Egypt, Moab, Syria, Edom, and Judea. Here all is plain and self-evident, as time has witnessed the fulfillment. But from that memorable event, the downfall of Jerusalem, on to a certain chronological period, called by Daniel *"the time of the end,"* all is obscurity. No interpretation breaks the seal of its wonders. Clouds curtain the heavens; and the symbols that glow in the vision of God's holy prophets are alike mysterious to them and to the wondering seraphim.

To Daniel, the prince of the prophets, this great truth seemed first to have been announced. When the prophet had the stupendous visions covering that symbolic period, he exclaimed: *"I heard, but I understood not: then said I, O my Lord, What shall be the end of these wonders? And he said, Go thy way, Daniel; for the words are closed up and sealed till the time of the end."* This positive declaration of Jehovah was thrice repeated to the prophet. But Gabriel gives him to understand personally thus much: These wonders will not occur in your day, Daniel; you will rest with your fathers long before the seal shall be broken; nevertheless, you will arise in the resurrection of the just; therefore, go thy way, and be comforted with the blessed hope. Such we suppose to be the meaning of the angel, when, closing his sublime mission to the prophet, he said, *"But go thou thy way till the end be: for thou shalt rest, and stand in thy lot in the end of the days."*

That the time of the end was a certain chronological length, and not the end of the world, is very certain, for things are said of the time of the end not at all consistent with the scriptural account of the day of judgment. In the time of the end *"many should run to and fro, and knowledge be increased;"* then *"the wise should understand, but none of the wicked should understand."* Whereas, in the final day, we suppose the wise and the wicked will both understand. These expressions evidently characterize that period called the time of the end, as an age of great locomotion, intelligence, and enterprise. And the words *"wise"* and *"wicked,"* being generic terms, and nouns of multitude, doubtless refer to nations. The friends of civil and religious liberty shall understand, but subjects of absolutism, and the dupes of despotism, shall not understand.

As the visions of Daniel, that covered the lapse of ages to the time of the end, were sealed and closed up, it is conclusive that the visions of Isaiah and Ezekiel, Jeremiah and John, embracing the same subjects and measuring the same period, are interdicted also. This is a legitimate and necessary deduction.

Now, is it not very surprising that eminent men, deeply pious and profoundly learned, have never discovered the *"seal"* of the Divine interdiction placed upon these visions? The impenetrable mystery, by Divine authority, hangs before their eyes, while the vague and unsatisfactory explanations of the most gifted commentators confirm the truth of the Divine prohibition. The truth is, there is not one writer in the long learned catalogue of commentators on the prophecies, down to our present theory, but has attempted to explain the meaning of these symbols by principles and rules that were known and applied during the interdicted ages, and are consequently necessarily erroneous; for God had again and again declared, *"the vision is sealed, and the words are closed up till the time of the end."*

Two obvious truths are here revealed: 1. The closing up of the vision down to a certain period. 2. As the sealing of the vision was only till that time, of course when that time should come the seal would be broken and the vision be understood.

If, therefore, the period when these sublime disclosures should be made was to be characterized **as an age of vast enterprise, intellectual energy, and moral adventure; and if we live in such an age** – an age marked with unparalleled progress and discovery – we ask, with the profoundest reverence, may we not venture to inquire, and to inquire hopefully, for the meaning of these wonders?

Should it be demanded, why have not the erudite and the learned in ages past apprehended this interpretation of prophecy, we have already anticipated the inquiry: that God had *sealed* a knowledge of these wonders during those ages. But should the unassuming pretensions of the learned author of Armageddon be looked upon as a barrier to a candid investigation of this most deeply interesting theory, we have only to suggest that great and ingenious minds are too magnanimous for such uncandid evasion. As the gifted author himself has asked, "May not a child find a gem?" Was it not a poor peon of the mountains that first discovered the riches of Peru? But perhaps one material reason why our great country has hitherto never been dreamed of as the burden of prophetic truth, has been owing to the fact that most of the principal writers on prophecy have been Englishmen, who putting one foot of the compasses down on Great Britain as the centre of creation, and describing a circle, have invariably left out the United States of America; somewhat after the fashion of a Chinese map of the world, which, after giving to the Celestial Empire almost the entire map, puts down Europe and America on a space no larger than a penny, calling them the "Barbarian Islands."

We will certainly be excused for disposing of another class of captious cavilers. It has been asked with much emphasis, "What good, or what purpose, could the truth of such a theory accomplish?" This inquiry, we will apprise you, is never made by the learned or the considerate; certainly not by one who reveres the truth of the Holy Scriptures.

What is the design of prophecy? Surely, wise and glorious accomplishments were intended by the Almighty in communicating to his servants the words and visions of prophecy. Doubtless, to inspire the hope of man for their realization, and to confirm the faith of mortals in the divinity of those truths by their fulfillment. But where will you find a broader field for such accomplishments, or a more glorious theatre for the fulfillment of prophetic truth, than in the providential rise and prosperity of a great nation that should be the exponent and example of popular freedom – a nation whose principles and progress should excite the admiration and arouse the emulation of the whole earth? Let men but behold, on this magnificent scale, a fulfillment of those sublime symbols and announcements that have staggered the philosophy of men, and baffled their profoundest learning from age to age; then indeed infidelity would seek annihilation for shelter, and its last refuge of lies be swept from the face of the earth.

We shall first consider the symbolic predictions of the United States.

The Time of Its Rise

The rise of a great nationality is evidently predicted by Daniel, when *"the power of the holy people,"* or friends of civil and religious liberty, shall **cease to be scattered;** when the wise nations should understand, and *"many should run to and fro, and knowledge be increased."* This glorious era was to be the period called *"the time of the end."* The rise of the United States of America synchronizes with that *"time,"* and no other nation under heaven.

The chronological argument is purely mathematical, and we believe unanswerable.

The decree of Cyrus for the emancipation of Israel was published in the last month of the year 537 B.C., (about December 6th), as is found by the coincidence of an eclipse of the sun, predicted by Thales the Milesian, that occurred B.C. 601, as well as the historic account of those ages. The crucifixion of Christ was on the 25th of March, A.D. 29, (Vulgar era), as found also by an eclipse of the moon and historic records. And the destruction of the Jewish state began on the 21st of Nisan, A.D. 68. The 70 weeks of Daniel were to begin at the decree of Cyrus, and to end at both the other named epochs. From the decree of Cyrus to the crucifixion was 564 years and 109 days; and from the same decree to the last general Jewish Passover was 603 years and 129 days. These two lengths were embraced in the 70 weeks, and show the precise duration of those weeks, as exactly those many years and days transpired to reach the events predicted. This fact no one can deny.

Now the explanation of the matter is simple: the 70 weeks are Hebrew weeks of years, or 490 years. But these are **abbreviated weeks**; that is, they require the addition of one or more kinds of sacred time to complete them. By adding the sabbatic days which would be in 490 years, we have 560 years. These are symbolic years of 360 parts; and as a symbolic year may stand for any Hebrew year of years, it may stand for the one of 364. Then we have the equation of time, as $360: 364 - 560: 566^2/_9$.

These $566^2/_9$ years are composed of 364 days each; and by reducing them to solar time of 365 days, 5 hours, 48 minutes, and $47^1/_{10}$ seconds to the year, we have 564 years and 109 days, as the fulfillment exhibits.

In a similar manner the other results will be found; but this example is a sufficient illustration of the principle of explaining sacred time.

The $3^1/_2$ times of *Daniel*, chapter 12, are, by this mode of explanation, easily understood. Three and a half times, or years, are equal to 1260 symbolic years. To this, if we add sabbatic years proportionably, we have 1440 years; and again adding proportionable sabbatic years, or one to every six, we have 1680 years. Then, as the symbolic year of 360 parts may represent any Hebrew year, it may represent the year 366 days or parts. We then have the following equation: $360: 366 \times 1680$ equals 1708 years, or 623,833 days, 17 hours, 1 minute, and 40 seconds.

These $3^1/_2$ times were to begin at the **cessation of the daily sacrifice**. The daily sacrifice was offered at sunrise. The sun arose at the meridian of Old Jerusalem on the 189th day of the year 68 A.D., about 5 o'clock A.M. This, then, is the beginning of the $3^1/_2$ times, or the 1260 symbolic days, or the

2300 *"evening mornings."* An *"evening morning"* was a lamb sacrifice at sunrise, and a lamb sacrifice at sunset – two lambs to a day; so 2300 are equal to 1150 days; add the proportion of sabbatic time, and 2300 evening mornings equal 3½ times. These lengths all agree, and embrace, in solar time, 623,833 days and 17 hours; and from the last Jewish sacrifice end at the meridian of Philadelphia, at a quarter to three o'clock in the afternoon of July the 4th, 1776.

Another length of these times is 1335 days, which, by the same rule, equal 1810 solar years, and will end in 1878. These two endings begin and close *"the time of the end,"* and answer to the rise of the American Republic and the expansion into the millennium. The 1290 and 1335 days coincide with the two lengths of the 3½ times.

In brief, Daniel's 70 symbolic weeks embrace the time from the decree of Cyrus to build and restore the city and temple, to the crucifixion of Christ and the final destruction of Jerusalem, which, in solar time, was 564 years to the first event and 603 years to the latter. And from this last event, the destruction of the holy place, it was to be 3½ times, or 623,833 days and 17 hours, to the rise of a great nationality.

Now, if 70 symbolic weeks are equal to 564 solar years, 3½ times, or 1260 symbolic days, are equal to 1708 solar years; but 1708 solar years, or 623,833 days, reach from the burning of the temple on the 189th day of the year 68, A.D., to the 4th day of July, 1776.

Let it be remembered, the 70 weeks call for two endings – the cutting off of Messiah, and the destruction of the holy place. But these two events are 39 years apart. The two lengths are made out legitimately by adding the proper sabbatic time of days, weeks, and years, as authorized by the Jewish calendar; for the weeks themselves are **"determined,"** **cut short or abbreviated weeks**. So that both lengths are accurately fulfilled, and are correctly termed *"70 weeks."*

But to suppose, as do most all of the old commentators, that a day means a year, and that 70 weeks are to be understood as 490 years, is to fall short of the events predicted, 94 years in the first case, and 113 years in the second; consequently, their theory is false. But time has not only demonstrated the error in their opinion of the 70 weeks, but also their error in relation to the 1260 and 1290 days that were to follow. If days meant years, pray tell us what great nationality arose at the end of the 1290 years after the destruction of Jerusalem? or what other great event happened that could possibly be construed into a fulfillment? Positively none.

The calculation, being purely mathematical, and guided by astronomy, has been rigidly made to the tenth fraction of a second, and must be reliable. The interpretation of the chronology is legitimate, for it is governed by Daniel's 70 weeks; consequently, the fulfillment is shown in the rise of a glorious civil and religious republic exactly at the end of these symbolic lengths, and that republic is the United States of America.

The fifth government in the dream of King Nebuchadnezzar, or the *stone kingdom,* symbolizes our great nationality.

The king of Babylon saw in his vision a vast image, *"whose brightness was excellent, and the form thereof was terrible. This image's head was of fine gold, his breast and his arms of silver, his belly and his thighs of brass, his legs of iron, his feet part of iron and part of clay."* In this terrific image, as interpreted by the prophet, God showed to the Assyrian monarch the whole of monarchy to the end of time, in four great dynasties that should consequently arise, his being the first of the series: *"Thou art this head of gold. After thee shall arise another kingdom inferior to thee,"* etc. It is universally admitted by the learned, that the Assyrian, the Medo-Persian, the Macedonian, and the Roman Empires, are clearly and unequivocally represented here, and that, too, in the order in which they arose.

In the fourth or iron portion of this image, another substance enters into the formation of its feet and toes, of which a more minute and extended description and the interpretation are given than of any other part of the dream: *"And whereas thou sawest the feet and toes, part of potters' clay, and part of iron, the kingdom shall be divided; and there shall be in it of the strength of the iron, forasmuch as thou sawest the iron mixed with the miry clay. And as the toes of the feet were part of iron, and part of clay, so the kingdom shall be partly strong, and partly broken. And whereas thou sawest iron mixed with miry clay, they shall mingle themselves with the seed of men; but they shall not cleave one to another, even as iron is not mixed with clay."* That the two materials constituting the feet and toes should always have been understood to represent a division of the kingdom into a stronger and weaker part of the civil government is the only opinion perhaps ever offered by commentators in every age.

The theory of Armageddon alone maintains that the division of the fourth empire, as represented by the feet and toes, symbolizes the ten kingdoms, which according to Bishop Newton, was the exact number that actually did arise from the old Roman empire; but that the iron and clay in the feet and toes symbolized the **union of Church and State,** and nothing else. With this interpretation the words of the angel perfectly agree, and are impressively intelligible: *"Whereas thou sawest iron mixed with miry clay,* **they shall mingle themselves with the seed of men; but they shall not cleave one to another,** *even as iron is not mixed with clay."* That is, as a perfect chemical amalgam with the two cannot be formed, because the ingredients will not adhere, so the union of Church and State will never be happy in its combination – never a harmonious and peaceful union – but an illegitimate commerce, unsanctioned by the will of God, and ruinous to the best interests of the human family. *"They shall mingle themselves with the seed of men."* That is, a superior order of men will join an in-ferior order; or the Church shall be joined to the State, and, consequently, such a government must always be partly strong and partly broken – a politico-ecclesiastical concubinage that would curse the nations of the earth.

This interpretation is greatly strengthened by the chronological character of the image, the iron and clay enter into the composition of the feet and toes, after that the Roman Empire for a thousand years had stood upon its iron legs, a nation of soldiers. The date of the feet synchronizes most wonderfully with the event represented; for Church and State union in the Roman Empire began under Constantine, A.D. 325, and was perpetuated with each of the ten-toed kingdoms that swarmed out of the old Roman hive.

Such was the image and its legitimate interpretation, a knowledge of which is essential to a correct understanding of the fifth or stone kingdom.

"Thou sawest till that a stone was cut out without hands, which smote the image upon his feet that were of iron and clay, and brake them to pieces. Then was the iron, the clay, the brass, the silver, and the gold, broken to pieces together, and became like the chaff of the summer threshing-floors; and the wind carried them away, that no place was found for them; and the stone that smote the image became a great mountain, and filled the whole earth."

Of this sublime symbol the angel gives the following interpretation: ***"In the days of these kings shall the God of heaven set up a kingdom, which shall never be destroyed;*** *and the kingdom shall not be left to other people, but it shall break in pieces and consume all these kingdoms, and it shall stand for ever. Forasmuch as thou sawest that the stone was cut out of the mountain without hands, and that it brake in pieces the iron, the brass, the clay, the silver, and the gold; the great God hath made known to the king what shall come to pass hereafter; and the dream is certain, and the interpretation thereof sure."* Let it be observed, the word *kingdom,* in the prophecies, is a convertible term with government, and must be so understood in this passage.

The absurdity of applying the stone kingdom to Christianity is so very obvious, it is indeed remarkable that the learned should endorse such an opinion. The stone could not symbolize Christianity, 1. Because it did not arise at the proper time for Christianity. *"In the days of these kings"* must refer to that plurality of kings last mentioned, the ten-toed kings or kingdoms, that arose from the Roman Empire. The philosophy of our language demands this sense. But Christianity arose in the days of one king, Augustus Caesar. In point of fact, then, the truth of history for ever forbids any other interpretation. Our great nationality arose exactly in the days of that very plurality of kings or kingdoms that came out of the old Roman dynasty. 2. The stone kingdom did not arise in the **proper place** for Christianity. Rome arose where the Grecian empire had stood, the Grecian or Macedonian succeeded Medo-Persia, and Medo-Persia was successor to the Babylonian or Assyrian kingdom; but the stone kingdom had no previous connection with this corporate image of monarchy; did not grow up under its shadow, precincts, or presence, but comes from a distance, and strikes the image from without, and, at one dreadful stroke of external violence, breaks the colossal image to fragments; and its atoms, ground to infinitesimal dust, fly like chaff before *"the winds of the summer threshing floors."* But Christianity arose within the dominions of Rome: Judea was a Roman province where Christianity was born. 3. The stone kingdom could not have arisen at all at the time that Christianity arose, or it would have risen in the Roman Empire also; for Rome at that time embraced the known world.

At the birth of Christ, *"There went out a decree from Caesar Augustus, that all the world should be taxed."* But there was a land, my countrymen, where the Roman cohorts were never marshaled – a land that Heaven had concealed from the cupidity and ambition of her conquering armies. **That land is our own beloved America, the only portion of the globe, beyond the limits of ancient Rome, where a great nationality, in its constitution, character, and mission, could possibly answer the true meaning of the fifth symbolic kingdom that the God of heaven would set up.**

As the political governments of monarchy were severally represented by a symbol taken from the mineral kingdom in one corporate connection, showing the uniformity of the genius that pervaded the whole, so the fifth government, being political also, is symbolized by a mineral type (a stone) likewise. But being entirely distinct from and unconnected with the image of monarchy, it is very clear that the fifth government is not only a political organization, but an anti-monarchical government; consequently, a political republican government, arising under the supervision of Almighty God . . . *"a stone cut out of the mountain **without hands**:"* brought into being a glorious nationality by a wonderful chain of Divine providences.

The violent destruction of the monarchical image by the stone necessarily implies political organizations and military power. The mild and tranquil genius of Christianity offers no violence to any man, or any nation; but it wins its gradual conquests by moral persuasion. But here is a power dreadful as the enginery of battle, swift and destructive as the bolt of heaven. And did Christianity indeed break down and annihilate the Roman Empire? What a failure! Was it not the barbarian hordes of Goths and Vandals from the North that overran imperial Rome? But how are we to account for the stone smiting the image *"on the feet?"* Why was the attack not made upon the head, or upon some vital part?

Let it be remembered, the feet was the point of the union of the Church and State; consequently, the mission of this great fifth nationality was the destruction of State and Church union, as well as the utter and ultimate extermination of ecclesiastical and political despotism from the face of the earth. Now, we appeal to the assembled wisdom before us, to profound statesmen, and venerable ministers of God, if the antagonism of the stone to the iron and clay is not fully answered in the genius of the American people? Are not the sentiment and feeling of this great nation more harmonious and universal in their hostility to Church and State union than on any other subject? Has not the Constitution of the United States, in devoting a whole chapter to the subject, raised an eternal barrier against it? And is not our nation the only enlightened government among the nations of the earth, where the illegitimate union of Church and State is most solemnly interdicted? thus leading our free people to *"Render unto Caesar the things which are Caesar's and unto God the things that are God's."*

While it is, therefore, conclusive that the **stone kingdom** is a providential political government, *"cut out of the mountain without hands,"* incompatible with, hostile to, and destined in its great mission to annihilate the last vestige of monarchy from the nations of the earth, it is equally evident that *"the mountain"* out of which the stone is cut **is Christianity.** So our great government is founded upon the Bible. Remove this indestructible basis that supports the fair fabric of our political institutions, and we have no government. The Declaration of American Independence evidently recognizes the obligations of the **first,** and fully embraces the principles of the **second** great commandment. The smiles of a Christian Sabbath inspire the devotion, and call from labor to rest our toiling millions; while the obligation of every officer of state, from the chief magistrate of the nation down to the humblest minister of justice, is rendered inviolate by a solemn averment upon Divine revelation.

The history of the world confirms the fact that a nation's religion moulds the character of its civic government. A despotic, superstitious, and blood-thirsty system of religion will form and fashion its political economy after the same model. So a pure, enlightened, and divinely authorized religion has ever been the maternal source of a pure, liberal, and happy civil government.

As, therefore, the four great empires were to be succeeded by a fifth great government, altogether differing in its principles and character, and as the United States of America is the only great nation that ever has or ever can arise to answer the description and fill the mission of the fifth empire, the conclusion is inevitable, **that our glorious republic is the stone kingdom that the God of heaven was to "set up."**

A glimpse of this sublime reality inspired the good Bishop Berkeley, more than a hundred years ago, to declare what even now seems a wonderful consummation:

> *"Westward the star of empire makes its way;*
> *The first four acts already passed,*
> *The fifth shall close the drama with the day;*
> *Time's noblest offspring is the last."*

The United States of America is symbolized by the man-child of the winged woman of the wilderness.

"And there appeared a great wonder in heaven; a woman clothed with the sun, and the moon under her feet, and upon her head a crown of twelve stars. And there appeared another wonder in heaven; and behold a great red dragon, having seven heads and ten horns, and seven crowns upon his heads . . . And the dragon stood before the woman which was ready to be delivered, for to devour her child as soon as it was born.

"And she brought forth a man-child, who was to rule all nations with a rod of iron; and her child was caught up to God, and to his throne . . . And to the woman were given two wings of a great eagle, that she might fly into the

wilderness, into her place . . . And the serpent cast out of his mouth water as a flood, that he might cause her to be carried away of the flood. And the earth helped the woman, and the earth opened her mouth, and swallowed up the flood which the dragon cast out of his mouth. And the dragon was wroth with the woman," etc.

It is almost universally admitted that the true Church of God is represented by the woman in this symbol. And, without pausing to examine the many opinions which divines have entertained as to the true meaning of the man-child – some supposing it refers to Christ, and others to Constantine – we will demonstrate that the symbolic meaning of the man-child is that of a great nationality that was to arise under the superintending providence of Almighty God in the latter times; and that that great nationality is the United States of America.

To this man-child a **rod** was given to **rule** – always the ensign of political power; so that, while the mother represents a pure, enlightened religion, her offspring, "a man-child," who is invested with political authority, must represent an enlightened nationality. This exposition we claim with great confidence to be legitimate. We shall now show that such is the testimony of the Holy Scriptures.

Isaiah declares, *"Before she travailed, she brought forth; before her pain came, she was delivered of a man-child. Who hath heard such things? who hath seen such things? Shall the earth be made to bring forth in one day? or shall **a nation be born at once?** for as soon as Zion travailed, she brought forth."*

In this passage, the *"Zion"* meaning the Church of God, settles, beyond all doubt, the symbolic meaning of the *"woman clothed with the sun;"* and as the *"man-child"* in the one case is put in apposition with *"a nation born at once,"* he must be understood in the other instance to be the symbol of a **nation** also. We cannot deny the explanation without denying the interpretation the Holy Scriptures give of their own symbols.

But is this nationality, arising from a true and enlightened religion, the United States of America? We shall see. In the first place, the man-child was the offspring of a true and enlightened religion. 2. Its destruction was determined upon, in its infancy, by a great red ragon. 3. It received *"a rod"* in its infancy, to rule, or to maintain political jurisdiction. 4. He and his mother were favored by the *"earth."* 5. *"The child was caught up to the throne of God."*

Now, how remarkably does our great nation answer to this description? Our nationality arose from and was the legitimate offspring of an enlightened liberal religion. Our honored ancestry, having fled from the storms of persecution in the old world, sought to find in the new, freedom to worship God; **the founders and framers of our political fabric being, in the main, worshipers of the true God, and believers in his Son Jesus Christ.**

Our infancy was warily watched by the demon of despotism, and fearful were the efforts made by the dragon of autocracy to crush us in the cradle. But *"the earth helped the woman."* The seat of the old Roman Empire is termed, in the symbolic language of the Apocalypse, "the earth." And did not several of the European powers come to our assistance in that dreadful conflict? Russia declared neutrality; Spain, and especially Holland, waged war against England, while the fleets of France came to our rescue in our Revolutionary struggle. "The earth helped the woman," and the man-child was rescued.

But we were specially protected and defended by the providence of Almighty God, which we understand the expression, *"caught up to the throne of God,"* to imply. How wonderful the eventful history of our new-born nation! Who can trace the special interventions of a Divine hand through all the stages of our infant existence, from our natal hour, without acknowledging that the God of Washington was on our side?

The coincidences are so numerous, and the agreement of our great nationality with the symbolic description of the man-child so wonderfully accurate, that the conclusion is demonstration. For if perfect coincidence be perfect fulfillment, then the United States of America is symbolized by the man-child of the winged woman in the wilderness.

The United States of America is the nationality that is promised in the prophetic Scriptures to arise in the latter times as *Israel Restored.* It has long been a favorite theory, both with Jewish and Christian writers, that the nationality to be gathered together in the latter days was understood to mean the returned or restoration of the scattered sons of Abraham to the land of Palestine. We are not surprised at the confidence with which this opinion has been entertained from age to age, because it is a legitimate *a priori* interpretation, seeing this nationality is called *"Israel"* by the prophets.

In a conversation had with a venerable Bishop of the Episcopal Church, he inquired of us: "Sir, by what construction of language do you make the great nationality, promised to arise in the latter times, to mean the United States? That the Bible authorizes us to expect such a nationality there can be no doubt; but how do you make out that nationality to be the United States of America, as it was promised to be Israel?" To which we replied: "Beloved Bishop, the predictions of the prophets are put up in Hebrew dress; the regalia is Mosaic, the custom is Israelitish. They did not say, friends of civil and religious liberty, Americans, or even Christians; but they used the best terms they had on hand: they said 'Israel.'"

Only doff the subject of its Jewish robes, and the symmetrical proportions and sublimity of Christian republicanism are as perfectly delineated as a Grecian pillar. But we will now show that what is reasonable and legitimate is a true principle of interpretation, being authorized by the great Teacher from heaven.

Said the disciples to our Lord, *"Why say the scribes that Elias must first come? for it is written, Behold, I will send Elijah the prophet, before that great and notable day of the Lord. Jesus answered and said unto them, Elias is come already, and they knew him not, but have done unto him whatsoever they listed. Then the disciples understood that he spake unto them of John the Baptist."*

Now, suppose the difficulty of the pious Bishop were proposed to our Lord: "Master, by what construction of language do you make out that **John the Baptist,** the son of Zacharias and Elizabeth, is indeed Elias the prophet, which was to come, seeing he is in reality another man altogether?" Does not the same difficulty exist in both cases; and has not our Lord, by answering the objection in one case, removed it in the other? John was *"the Elias which was for to come,"* not because that was the name by which he was called in his generation among men, but because he came *"in the spirit and power of Elias,"* thereby answering the moral portrait that was drawn by the pencil of inspiration, and was, consequently, declared by the Saviour to be indeed the Elias.

If, therefore, a great nationality is promised to arise in the latter days, and the United States of America exhibits the character of such nationality, as delineated by the pen of prophecy, arising *"in the spirit and power"* of Israel to come, and no other nation under heaven ever has or ever can answer the description, **then, perfect coincidence being perfect fulfillment, our glorious republic is the nationality which was to be gathered together in the latter times under the prophetic name of Israel.**

Let it be remembered, that the term Israel was a cognomen of honor, and not the natural right of a Jew. God gave the appellation to Jacob, because *"as a prince he prevailed with God."* While the children of Jacob maintained their integrity, they enjoyed this high distinction; but St. Paul defends the application of the term to Gentiles who may possess the proper claims to this honor.

But perhaps the most plausible bill of exceptions taken to our theory is presented here. It is suggested, with much apparent reason, that we are too wicked and unworthy a people to bear the honored title of Israel. Alas for us, my countrymen! Heaven knows full well we are wicked enough; for when we consider the special providence of Almighty God, marvelously exercised over us from the very infancy of our organization, through every change of fortune – what prosperity has crowned our cause – how we have been guided and guarded by a Divine supervision, as virtually present as the **holy Shekinah,** *"in a cloud by day, and a pillar of fire by night"* – and then look at the abominations that pollute our national escutcheon, it is humiliating in the extreme.

Look at the blasphemy that outrages the highest obligation of created beings, marring the purest language on earth, in desecrating the name of the holiest Being in the universe. Look at the violation of the heathen, discrediting honest character in almost all gradations of society. See the frenzy of political parties, disrupting the very bonds of brotherhood; while blood and debauchery infect the air and pollute the earth; bribery, homicide, and murder transpire in the very halls of our nation's councils.

But bad as we are, fellow-citizens, we are the very best people upon the face of the earth. The great heart of our magnanimous country beats responsive to the sighs and sorrows of all nations. Our peaceful land is the hospitable home for the oppressed of all countries. Our laws are the transcript of eternal justice. True, we have neither titled dukes nor hereditary lords, but the emoluments of profit and honor are offered to the deserving of all classes, and our loftiest promotions are accessible to the humblest poor. Though denounced abroad by all aristocracy that dooms its own pauper millions to proscription, beggary, and starvation, yet our institutions, which they fain would pity, are the pulsations of health, compared with the plague-spots of pestilential Europe.

Already have three hundred thousand of our African population become the Christianized children of God – a greater number of true Christian converts, heathens as their fathers were who first came amongst us, than are to be found in all the missions of all denominations upon the earth. We have colonized a happy republic also, upon the benighted shores of their fatherland. Our ministers of mercy have gone to every heathen shore, and preached glad tidings to almost every island that dots the bosom of the ocean. Beams of light, radiating from this central home of civil and religious liberty, already break upon the distant millions that weep in the shadow of death.

When the noble Greek is crushed by the hoof of Turkish despotism, the halls of our Senate are eloquent with a sympathy that responds in the bosom of a whole people. When Poland, Hungary, and Italy struggle and fall, the hope of the American people struggles and falls with them. When the cry of starvation is heard from ill-fated Ireland, American transports are freighted with the numificent offering of a generous people. And, moved by a magnanimity which knows no parallel, our swift ships are dispatched to recover England's lost navigators in the regions of eternal snow.

We have the one living and true God, one Saviour, and one religion – one Constitution, one Confederacy, one Republic, one nationality; **therefore, a true religion and a true civil government is the Israel that was to come, the "nation born at once" – born on the 4th of July, 1776.**

But let us not be misled by the consecrated name of Israel. For *"all are not Israel who are called Israel."* A nation possessing the true religion, and enjoying an enlightened and liberal civil government, may have many unbelieving and rebellious people in its midst; and, doubtless, millennial glory, and the day of judgment also, will find both the righteous and the wicked, the just and the unjust, the wise and the foolish virgins, for the wheat and tares will grow together until the general harvest, *"which is the end of the world."* Even Israel restored to nationality will not be the Eden of bliss.

It was in the brightest day of the Hebrew nation when the tribes of Jacob were led out to the solitudes of the desert to behold the glory of God revealed upon the sacred mountain. Clouds of awful grandeur encircled its brow. Lightnings rent the mantle of the sky, and deep-toned thunders rocked Mount Sinai from its glowing summit to its granite base. Then, where was Israel – God's own Israel? Behold him at the foot of the hill making a **golden calf!**

By the term of Israel, therefore, we mean to be understood, a providential nation, possessing the only true religion, and a divinely sanctioned form of civil government. Such, with all its sunshine and shadows, was ancient Israel, and such is the United States of America, and the United States of America alone.

As to the scattered Jews – who have long since lost all geneological proof of their respective tribes – forming such great nationality any where, that is supremely ridiculous. That they may return to Jewry, we think highly probable; because every thing formerly connected with that nation was typical. Their fiftieth, or Jubal year, was a time when the scattered Jews returned to their respective homes, and were put in possession or seized their patrimonial estates. This custom may anticipate the jubilee of the world; that is, when republicanism shall become world-wide.

Then the Jews, in masses, may return to Canaan; for the Almighty by deed of gift made Abraham and his posterity proprietors of that land. They may return and form a little Christian republic in Palestine. But to become the great national headship of the world, restore temple worship and priestly offerings, with all the gorgeous paraphernalia of its ancient sacerdotal splendor, is but the pious dream of fanaticism. This simplicity and spirituality of the religion of the Son of God forbids the idea; while the burdensome rites of the Jewish ritual have long since been discarded by the unostentatious loveliness and grace of a Christianity that claims to worship the Father *"in spirit and in truth."*

But even the supposition that they will return and form a literal government in their ancient home may be a mistake. For those prophecies that seem to refer to their literal restoration are interpreted by many worthy divines to foretell their conversion of their long-rejected Saviour. This is indeed plausible.

> **"In foreign climes they'll cease to roam'**
> **Nor weeping, think on Jordan's flood;**
> **In every land they'll find a home,**
> **In every temple worship God."**

And so must it be. But if the Almighty designed to honor a people by raising them to become a great nationality, of whom is it probable such nationality would be composed? Let this question be settled by a plain principle of Divine revelation. Who are the Jews? A persecuted and disbanded people. Why are they persecuted? For rejecting the claims of the Son of God. From His very birth to this day they have, as a nation, derided and discarded Him. They sealed the dreadful imprecation at His crucifixion: *"His blood be upon us, and on our children."*

But there is another persecuted people – the friends of civil and religious liberty. They have been hunted down in every land, like the hart of the mountains. They have been proscribed and execrated, outraged and banished, in every age; and, for conscience' sake, have been martyred by the millions. Why were they persecuted, *"scattered, and peeled?"* For accepting and acknowledging Jesus Christ. Here, then, is the difference. Now, apply an infallible principle which must test this question. Said the adorable Saviour, *"If any man serve me, him will my Father honor."*

Is it, then, at all probable that God would honor a people by the promised glorious nationality, who have, as a nation, spurned the mercy of the Prince of peace, and obstinately persisted, before the eyes of all nations, in rejecting the clearest evidence of His Messiahship, during the long, long night of their wanderings; and yet, at the same time, pass by a people who, through every change of fortune, propitious and adverse, have firmly maintained their faith in Christ, and invincibly breasted the storms of persecuting vengeance for His glorious name's sake? Will heaven honor a people who dishonor His Son, and over-look a people who were ready to live and labor and suffer and die in His blessed cause? The case being self-evident, and the rule to determine our judgment infallible, the deci-sion must be inevitable.

Christianity mourns the ill-fated children of a divinely chosen and illustrious ancestry, and ardently prays for their conversion to Christ. But even this glorious consummation our faith beholds far in the distance. That the Jews will ultimately embrace Christianity, we entertain no doubt; but they will be the last nation on the face of the earth that will be converted. For *"the blindness that has happened to Israel"* will remain *"until the fulness of the Gentiles is brought in."* That is, the Gentile world will be converted to God before the blindness of infidelity will be removed from Israel. To suppose the conversion of the Jewish nation to be the means of converting the Gentile world, is, consequently, directly opposed by the words of the apostle. In their case we behold the verification of another gospel maxim: *"the first shall be last, and the last first."* They were the first to hear the blessed tidings of man's redemption from the lips of its glorious Author, *"but they received him not."*

And the Apostle Paul, in his valedictory to his own countrymen, declares, *"seeing that ye judge yourselves unworthy of eternal life, lo, we turn to the Gentiles."* So, also, the melting strains that mingled with the tears of the Son of God over their devoted city announced the same calamity. *"O Jerusalem, Jerusalem, thou that killest the prophets, and stonest them which are sent unto thee; how often would I have gathered thy children together even as a hen gathereth her chickens under her wing, and ye would not . . . If thou hadst known, even thou, the things which belong unto thy peace, at least in this thy day, but now are they hid from thine eyes . . . Henceforth is your house left unto you desolate; for I say unto you, ye shall not see me henceforth till ye shall say, Blessed is he that cometh in the name of the Lord."* That is, Ye shall see me no more until you will be rejoiced to hail me as your Messiah. This is, doubtless, its true meaning.

There are very many passages of Scripture which are universally admitted by the learned and judicious to foretell the rise of a great nationality in the latter times. These predictions cannot, by any reasonable construction, be applied to the rise of such nationality in the land of Judea; but are most wonderfully descriptive of the United States of America, and of no other country under heaven.

We shall now select a few out of the many marked descriptions and coincidences only realized in our favored land and nation.

First. The land of the promised nationality was to be located _between two seas_ – the eastern sea and the great western sea: *"From the border unto the east sea, this is the east side . . . . The west side also shall be the great sea; from the border, this is the west side."* (Ezekiel 47:18,20) These broad boundaries of our great country are perfect; the west side being the *"great sea"* is most remarkable. Judea is not bounded on the east side by a sea at all. This passage, which is taken from the prophet's geographical description of the land of restored Israel, cannot possibly apply to Palestine, if Ezekiel has given its true boundaries. All commentators understand this chapter as an inspired account that maps the country of the promised nationality; but it is absolutely impossible to locate this land in Palestine, for the want of an eastern border. No sea bounds old Canaan on the east. Learned men have generally supposed that Palestine is the country referred to, but let learned men show us that eastern boundary. This *defect* is **fatal,** and must for ever vitiate the claim of Judea to this high distinction.

Second. This land is described as being hitherto uncultivated and unimproved – a land *"that has always been waste."* (Ezekiel 38) Of course Palestine cannot be referred to here, for it cannot be said in truth that Judea has always been waste. But our own country fully answers the description. Our primeval prairies and grand old woods presented, on the arrival of our ancestors, the same unbroken wilderness they had remained for ages, as though Heaven had specially preserved them for the glory of their future destiny. Let it not be said that the footprints of the aborigines of this country are an objection to this account; for that land is waste where tillage has never harvested its blessings for man. But such is the desert description of the country to be possessed by the nationality to come, and such was the new continent of America.

The song of the eloquent Isaiah can remind you of no other country: *"the wilderness and the solitary place shall be glad for them; and the desert shall rejoice, and blossom as the rose. It shall blossom abundantly, even with joy and singing: the glory of Lebanon shall be given unto it, the excellency of Carmel and Sharon, they shall see the glory of the Lord and the excellency of our God . . . For in the wilderness shall waters break out, and streams in the desert. And the parched ground shall become a pool, and the thirsty land springs of water: in the habitation of dragons, where each lay, shall be grass with reeds and rushes."*

Third. That wonderful country was to be inhabited by the people *"gathered out of the nations."* (Ezekiel 38) Not of one nation collected together that had been scattered amongst other nations, but, what is obviously the sense of the passage, composed of people of different nations. This is so prominent a character of the glorious nationality to come, that the prophets seem to dwell upon it with rapture and inspired eloquence. *"Lift up thine eyes round about, and see; all they gather themselves together, they come to thee: thy sons shall come from far, and thy daughters be nursed by thy side. Then thou shalt see, and flow together and thy heart shall fear, and be enlarged; for the abundance of the sea shall be converted* [turned] *unto thee, the forces of the Gentiles shall come unto thee . . . Who are these that fly as a cloud, and as doves to their windows?"*

The prophet enriches his sublime description by images drawn both from the animal and the vegetable kingdom: *"The multitude of camels shall cover thee, the dromedaries of Midian and Ephah; all they from Sheba shall come . . . . All the flocks of Kedar shall be gathered together unto thee . . . . The glory of Lebanon shall come unto thee, the fir tree, the pine tree, and the box together."* (Isaiah 60) As if the holy seer had said, emigration shall come from the land where the dromedaries roam; they shall come from the land where the fir tree blooms. *"Therefore thy gates shall be open continually; they shall not be shut day nor night."*

Did ever such a tide of emigration set into any country since the creation of the world as continually swarms to our hospitable shores? Indeed, the citizens of these States, or their fathers, have come from almost every country under heaven. But the prophet enters into detail. *"Strangers shall stand and feed your flocks, and the sons of the alien shall be your ploughmen and your vinedressers . . . And the sons of strangers shall build your walls, and their kings shall minister unto thee."* Now, the walls of a country's defence are its public improvements; and it is notorious that the sons of strangers build most of our public works.

"The sons also of them that afflicted thee shall come bending unto thee; and all they that despised thee shall bow themselves down at the soles of thy feet." The sons of the very soldiers that invaded your coasts, murdered your people, and burnt your towns and villages, should come to make your country their home; and those who sneered at your experiment of popular freedom, attempted to crush it in the cradle, predicted the downfall of American Independence, and that liberty would die with Washington, and with his dust receive the same rites of sepulture – yes, even they should come and seek a refuge and a home in your happy land. How imposing the picture drawn by the pencil of inspiration here; and how wonderfully true is the fulfillment.

Fourth. In the promised nationality, unlike the political economy of ancient Israel, foreigners were to be allowed a place to dwell, enjoy their homes and the pursuits of happiness, in common with the citizens of the country; but it seems from the prophet, the rights of suffrage and eligibility of office were only to be enjoyed by those strangers who had lived long enough in the land to raise their native-born children: *"And it shall come to pass, that ye shall divide it by lot for an inheritance unto you,* **and to the strangers that sojourn among you, which shall beget children among you; and they shall be unto you as born in the country among the children of Israel; they shall have inheritance with you among the tribes of Israel** *. . . And in what tribe the stranger sojourneth, there shall ye give him his inheritance, saith the Lord God."* (Ezekiel 47:22,23)

There could be no propriety in characterizing the class of foreigners who should be blessed with children born in the land, from the stranger who is only a sojourner, whose residence is but recent and transient, unless peculiar privileges were understood to belong to the fathers of native-born children. As we lay no claims to the politician, we will be allowed strongly to approve of this interesting feature in the economy of restored Israel. Our land should always be the welcome home of foreigners; but, at the same time, they should remain long enough to appreciate our blessings, learn our laws, and the genius of our wonderful constitution, before they aspire to dictate or to govern.

Fifth. The principle of *extension*, in enlarging the boundaries of their primary possessions should specially characterize the prosperity of the promised nationality.

"Lift up thine eyes round about, and behold: all these gather themselves together, and come to thee . . . For thy waste and desolate places shall even now be too narrow, by reason of the inhabitants, and they that swallowed thee up [the autocracy of the Old World] *shall be far away* [beyond the sea]. *The children which thou shalt have* [in this land], *after thou hast lost the other* [ancient Israel], *shall say again in thy ears, The place is too strait for me: give place to me that I may dwell."* (Isaiah 49:18,20)

Extension seems to be the genius of our free institutions. From thirteen States, we have already multiplied into thirty-one, besides nine territories that soon will be ready to enter into the Union.

We need give ourselves no uneasiness about Mexico, Cuba, and Central America. Monarchy and anarchy must melt away in the immediate proximity of a glorious republic: while the natural interests of those countries will impel them to seek annexation, that they may also enjoy in common with us the benign blessings of our happy confederacy. Indeed, the words of prophecy, legitimately interpreted, warrant that the domain of this nationality will embrace the entire continent of North and South America. For its *"dominion shall be from sea to sea, and from the river unto the ends of the earth."* We know this passage is usually applied to Christ, to which we make no objection. But will you restrict it to him? If so, you greatly diminish the universal triumphs of his reign. We are taught that his sway shall be illimitable, and every knee shall bow and pay homage to him.

But the passage before us is a clear territorial grant, issued by Divine authority, and must mark the boundaries of Israel that was to come. The geographical description can be found applicable to no other country but ours. Here the grant finds all of its metes and bounds. *"From sea to sea;"* from the Atlantic to the Pacific Ocean. *"And from the river:"* the Mississippi, the father of waters, with its sixty thousand miles of tributary navigation, and the incalculable tonnage of its transports. *"Unto the ends of the earth:"* to the most remote promontories in the North, and to Terra del Fuego and Cape Horn in the South. We must be excused from dwelling further on the emigration that was to come to this land. These predictions are very numerous and wonderfully accurate – inspired predictions, that never have been realized, and never can be unless they are fulfilled in the New World. We will, however, notice one other.

"Behold, these shall come from far; and, lo, these from the North and from the West; and these from the land of Sinim." (Isaiah 49:12) Now, all commentators agree that *"Sinim"* is China. The fact is, it was its true ancient name: **Thinim, Thina,** or **China.** It is so put down in the ancient maps. And China lies "north" and "west," or north-west of us. In the message of Ex-Governor Bigler, of California, some two years ago, it is there published that there were then some sixty thousand Chinese in that State. Now, no commentator questions that this passage describes emigration coming to the land of restored Israel, for the whole continent confirms it. But how are the Chinese to come from China to Palestine and come from the **north-west?** It is impossible. Here is a promise made of emigration from a distant country, whose

inhabitants have never been known to mingle with other nations; here their true ancient name is given; here is the very direction which they were to come; and here is a fulfillment upon a most magificent scale. Perfect coincidence being perfect fulfillment, our position is demonstration.

Sixth. The land of restored Israel is described as a country **restored from its desolations, by the peculiar construction of its towns and villages, and the prosperity and quietude of its inhabitants.**

In the invasion of this land, at the last great battle, by Russia, and the autocracy of the Old World, the prophet thus addresses the power that leads that invasion: *"After many days thou shalt be visited: thou shalt come into the land that is gathered out of many people, against the mountains of Israel, which have been always waste; but it is brought out of the nations, and they shall dwell safely all of them . . . Thou shalt say, I will go up to the land of unwalled villages; I will go to them that are at rest, that dwell safely, all of them dwelling without walls, and having neither bars nor gates. To take a spoil, and to take a prey; to turn thy hand upon the desolate places that are now inhabited, and upon the people that are gathered out of the nations; which have gotten cattle and goods, that dwell in the midst of the land."* (Ezekiel 38:8,11,12)

Here, my countrymen, is almost a daguerreotype portraiture of your own land. We very much question whether Ezekiel the prophet ever saw an *"unwalled"* city in his life. Surely, if old Palestine is to be brought back again to her more than ancient splendor, *"unwalled"* cities and villages will not be found there. This passage, therefore, can never be applied to Judea; for all her cities were walled, from Jericho to Jerusalem. **This remarkable description of the numerous villages and cities, and the possessions, prosperity, and security of the people, is a grand and graphic delineation of the United States of America, and of no other country on earth.**

Seventh. The infancy of that country should receive the atttention of royal patronage: *"Kings shall be thy nursing fathers, and queens thy nursing mothers."* How very remarkably this has been realized will occur to the mind at once. The term *"nursing"* applies to infancy. And it was at the early history of our people that the supervision of royalty was exercised over us. The names of several of the old thirteen States, besides many counties and towns, still perpetuate the recollection of royalty: Georgia and Virginia, Maryland and the Carolinas, as well as King and Queen and King William counties, Prince George, Prince Edward, and prince we don't know what else – names that will for ever perpetuate the fulfillment of prophecy in what might otherwise seem to be only accidental.

Eighth. A country remarkable for the number of its majestic rivers.

"But there the glorious Lord will be unto us a place of broad rivers and streams; wherein shall go no galley with oars, neither shall gallant ship pass thereby." (Isaiah 33:21) This passage from the prophet is admitted to refer to the land of restored Israel. But if that land be Palestine, how are we to see the force of its meaning? Can the river Jordan and the rivulet Kedron answer the grandeur of this description? Certainly not. But the many mighty and majestic rivers in our own country fill up the prophetic map upon a sublime and magnificent scale. By the expression *"there the glorious Lord will be unto us a place of,"* etc., we understand that He will guarantee that description of country to the nation He would raise up. *"Wherein shall go no galley with oars,"* is very singular. The Hebrew word translated *"galley,"* literally signifies a **government clipper,** sent out by a superior kingdom to exact port-duties from a dependent people. The loss of the tea cargo in Boston harbor fully illustrates this subject; while the very genius of our independence, in the days of Andrew Jackson, was stamped upon a medal: **"Millions for defence, but not one cent for tribute."**

Ninth. The land of restored Israel is described to be literally *more elevated* than any portion of the world.

"The mountain of the Lord's house shall be established upon the tops of the mountains, and all nations shall flow unto it." The willful king of the North says in his proclamation of war against us: *"I will go up to the land of unwalled villages."* Lieutenant Maury has shown, in one of his late learned works, that the **United States of America is the highest part of the visible earth,** and that it is down stream from the ports of our country to every other continent and island of the globe. But if this elevation must be morally and intellectually understood, and not literally, still, the realization being as perfect in the one case as in the other, our argument remains conclusive.

Tenth. The peaceful character of the inhabitants, and the intelligibility and uniformity of their language, should designate that people.

"Thou shalt not see a fierce people, of a deeper speech than thou canst perceive; of a stammering tongue, that thou canst not understand." (Isaiah 33:19)

Polite manners and gentle deportment every where characterize the American people: this is a world-wide acknowledgment, so that the solitary exceptions are gloated over by the detracting prints of roving authors as morsels too precious to be erased from their journals. But the uniformity and intelligibility of our language is indeed most extraordinary. Although teeming thousands are constantly pouring into our communities from the Germanic States, France, and other countries, our pure vernacular Anglo-Saxon will conduct you safely through any portion of our vast domain. And it is now contended, by those competent to judge, that the English is more correctly spoken in the wilds of America than at the court of St. James – more accurately pronounced in our primary schools than in the British Parliament. We do not question their intelligence nor their energy, but Americans speak the

English language better than the English themselves. Should the pride of an Albion tempt him to deny it, just put him upon his trial with any word where the consonant *"h"* is to be supplied or omitted – the monosyllable hell, for instance – and if he be not satisified with an attempt to spell and pronounce it, you may give him up as incorrigible.

Eleventh. The rapid advancement of **intelligence** and **divine instruction** should mark the rising progress of that people.

"Many shall run to and fro, and knowledge be increased." "All thy children shall be taught of the Lord, and great shall be the peace of thy children." What nation presents such a spectacle at this very moment as the United States? Our literary institutions are scattered all over the land, so that the humblest poor may be enriched with the treasures of science; while millions of sheets in the republic of letters pour floods of light upon the human mind. Here the press is free, that mighty enginery of thought, guarding the majesty of law and the inviolable sanctity of the Constitution. Here the pulpit, unawed by the terrors of the throne or the thunders of the Vatican, in tones of power and tongues of flame, procaims *"the acceptable year of the Lord,"* and preaches glad tidings to the poor. Here the word of God is an unchained book; and, like the sun in mid-heaven, rifts the clouds that mantle the world, shedding a strong and steady light upon the shadowy mansions of the dead, inspiring the living with the ecstatic hope that our loved and our lost shall awake from their dusty beds in the last glorious morning.

Twelfth. The country inhabited by the people *"gathered out of the nations"* should be settled in **thirteen distinct States,** like as it was with Israel: only *"Joseph should have two portions."*

"Ye shall inherit the land according to the twelve tribes of Israel: Joseph shall have two portions."

(Ezekiel 47:13) It is a remarkable fact that although the Jews had but twelve tribes, the portion falling to Ephraim and Manasseh, children of Joseph, being divided, made them a confederacy of thirteen states or tribes. It is also just as remarkable, that in the beginning we had but twelve States; and William Penn held the charter of Pennsylvania for twenty years before he obtained that of Delaware, and then we had thirteen States also. But the coincidence in the boundaries of the thirteen states of restored Israel with those of the old thirteen United States, is still more remarkable. The prophet gives the eastern border of each tribe to the **eastern sea,** and the western border of each tribe to be the **great western sea** (see Ezekiel 47). Wilson, and perhaps Bancroft, affirm, that the original charters of the thirteen United States called for the Atlantic or eastern ocean for their eastern boundary, and the Pacific or the great western ocean for their western boundary, in almost so many words.

It is not a little amusing to see the perplexity of the great and good Dr. Clarke, in attempting to map the land of restored Israel. He lays his plot, of course, in the territory of old Palestine. He bounds his thirteen lots by the Mediterrean or western ocean, but, for the life of the learned Doctor, he can find no **eastern sea** for his eastern border. The little Dead Sea lies across three of the tribes but does not bound any one of them! Examine his map, at the close of his commentary on Ezekiel, and you will find, **for want of an eastern sea, ancient Judea can never be the country of Israel restored.**

Thirteenth. Our country is the land described by the prophet Isaiah **lying westward from Judea.**

"Woe to the land shadowing with wings, which is beyond the rivers of Ethiopia, that sendeth messengers by the sea, even in vessels of bulrushes, saying, Go, ye swift messengers, to a nation scattered and peeled, to a people terrible from their beginning hitherto; a nation meted out

and trodden down, whose land the rivers have spoiled."
(Isaiah 18:1,2)

The word *"woe"* is not a malediction here, being **hoi erets** in Hebrew, a particle of hailing; and authorized us to read, ***"All hail,** thou land shadowing with wings."* But where is that land? From Judea, the stand-point of the prophet, it is *"beyond the rivers of Ethiopia."* Where are the rivers of Ethiopia? The Nile and its tributaries. What country and what people do we find beyond the Nile from Judea? The land is a barren desert, and the wandering Bedouins the only human beings that pass through it. Then we must look for another country and another people, but in the **same direction,** for that is specific. You will find no other land or people on that line of latitude until you strike the United States of America about the coasts of Carolina.

Should it be contended that Western Africa was not the ancient Ethiopia, but the country inhabited by the Cushites or the children of Cush, very well; they extended eastwardly until the Ganges, the Indus, and the Burrampooter were their rivers; and beyond these from Judea you come direct to the North American continent across the Pacific. So that, in either case, *"the land beyond the rivers"* of modern or ancient Ethiopia from Judea is America. Its description – *"a land shadowing with wings"* – might refer to the geographical conformation of the new continent, for a large map of North and South America very much resembles the expanded wings of a great eagle; or it may be suggestive of the fact that it was the country shadowed or concealed from the cupidity of the nations till God was ready for its discovery. Or was it not designed as a description of a country, the national aegis of whose people should be an eagle, whose pinions should spread from shore to shore? The *"swift ships"* and *"vessels of bulrushes"* are peculiarly descriptive of our fleets of commerce, as light water-crafts of this material were anciently used upon the Nile.

This land was originally possessed by *"a people hitherto terrible from the beginning."* Such is a true description of the fierce and warlike aborigines who were found in this new world. *"A people scattered and peeled:"* broken up into numerous tribes, dispersed without order over the whole country, and wasted by continual wars, were fast waning and melting away. *"Meted out and trodden down:"* driven from one part of the country to another, first located in one defined territory and then in another; oppressed, maltreated, and murdered. *"Whose land the rivers have spoiled:"* they being the original claimants and proprietors of a country extensive in its domain and rich in its alluvial lands, through which majestic rivers are ever changing their mighty channels.

This prophetic delineation of our country can have no other meaning or application. And learned commentators, never having dreamed that America was the subject of prophecy, acknowledge as does Dr. Adam Clarke, especially, "that this is the most obscure passage in the whole book of Isaiah." Our interpretation is certainly legitimate; while the facts and the fulfillment should awaken our attention and enkindle our admiration.

Fourteenth. But the promised nationality was to be a *republic*.

"Their nobles shall be of themselves, and their governor shall proceed from the midst of them." (Jeremiah 30:21) The people should be *"gathered together, and appoint unto themselves one head."* (Hosea 1:11) *"I will restore thy judges as at the first, and the counsellors as at the beginning."* (Isaiah 1:26) Observe *"one head"* – a chief magistrate appointed by the people – governors, judges, and counsellors, taken from the masses of the people, are particularly promised, but no king.

The political economy of ancient Israel being a theocratic republic, the promise in the passages is that the officers necessary to constitute a republican form of government would be restored, and the elective franchise would be free, and the people would possess the sovereign right of choosing their own rulers and judges. Surely the doctrine of the Divine right of kings finds no authority here; for the power invested in the people is entirely inconsistent with any grade of monarchy, limited or absolute.

The truth is, the **fifth** great commonwealth that the God of heaven was to "set up" was so *utterly repugnant to monarchy,* in all its forms and phases, that it should destroy it from the face of the earth. And we have every assurance that if the Almighty designed to bless a people by conferring upon them a particular form of political government, such form could not possibly be a monarchy.

A most memorable instance of Divine disapprobation of the establishment of an earthly king among men is recorded at the coronation of the first monarch of Israel. Said Almighty God to Samuel the prophet, *"**Protest solemnly** unto them, and show unto them the manner of the king that shall reign over them. He will take your sons, and appoint them for his chariots, and to be his horsemen; and some shall run before his chariots. And he will take your daughters to be confectionaries, and to be cooks, and to be bakers. And he will take your fields, and your vineyards, and your oliveyards, even the best of them, and give them to his servants. And he will take the tenth of your seed, and of your vineyards, and give them to his officers, and to his servants.*

"And he will take your men-servants, and your maid-servants, and your goodliest young men, and your asses, and put them to work. He will take the tenth of your sheep; and ye shall be his servants. And ye shall cry out in that day because of your king, and the Lord will not hear you in that day." (I Samuel 8:9-18)

Such is the solemn protestation of the God of heaven against an earthly monarchy; and faithfully has the history of earthly kings confirmed the truth of the Divine prediction. Then it is absolutely certain that a political government, selected and "set up" for the sons of men by Jehovah, would not be a monarchy. But this very fifth government was to be "set up" by the God of heaven; therefore the fifth government, not being in any possible case a monarchy in any grade, must be a republic.

Fifteenth, and finally. The **waiting isles** of Isaiah are a sublime announcement of our great country, and its early occupation by European emigrants. *"Surely, the isles shall wait for me, and the ships of Tarshish first, to bring my sons from far, their silver and their gold with them, unto the name of the Lord thy God, and to the Holy One of Israel."*

Diodorus Siculus, a most reliable historian of the Augustine age, says that "the term 'isles' in his time, primarily meant undiscovered lands supposed to exist in the Atlantic Ocean." The word "Tarshish," according to Strabo, refers to Tartesus, formerly a seaport city of that name, situated on the site where Cadiz now stands, in Old Spain, near the pillars of Hercules. And Mr. Benson, perhaps the most accurate commentator on the ancient geography of the Scriptures, says that "this opinion is now generally adopted by the learned."

With this explanation of terms, let us read the passage: **"Surely, the undiscovered lands in the western sea shall wait for me, and the ships of Old Spain shall be first to bring my sons from far, their silver, and their gold with them,"** etc.

Here we have the fact announced, that the country spoken of had hitherto been an undiscovered country, and the reason assigned why it should have remained concealed so long – *"shall wait for me"* – unknown and unexplored, until God, in his supervision of the nations, was ready for its occupation. *"Wait for"* God, until the Reformation in Europe had neutralized the friends of civil and religious liberty: until the great principle of self-government should move the masses of the people to seek a new theatre to realize the blessings of popular freedom – wait until the facilities of intellectual and moral improvement, the invention of printing, and the freedom of the pulpit, should arise as the powerful auxiliaries of an enlightened republican nation.

"And the ships of Old Spain shall be first, to bring my sons from far." And were not the ships of Spain first in the discovery and opening up of emigration to the New World? After being repulsed from every court in Europe to which he appealed, was not Columbus sanctioned and sustained by Ferdinand and Isabella in his expedition? *"To bring my sons from far."* Now, remember this passage cannot apply to the spread of the gospel, for the tidings of salvation are sent out to heathen lands; but here the sons of God are represented as being transported from their original homes to a newly discovered country. It cannot refer to Judea, for that was not an undiscovered country, and the ships of Spain never have brought, and never can bring, its first emigration to people it. *"Their silver and their gold with them:"* that they might make that land their permanent home, bringing their treasure with them.

But the great motive of their emigration deserves special attention. **They were to come for the privilege of worshipping God *"unto the name of the Lord thy God, and to the Holy One of Israel."*** Our noble ancestry, driven by the storms of persecution from the Old World, sought a refuge in the New. When the minions of monarchy invaded the Southern hemisphere, it was for the sake of gold. The Portugese in Brazil, Cortez in Mexico, and Pizarro in Peru, took possession of those countries in the names of the majesties of their respective governments. But when the Huguenots, the Quakers, and the Puritans came to America, they took possession of these lands in the name of Almighty God.

"Not as the conquerors come,
  They the true-hearted came:
  Not with the roll of the stirring drum,
  Or the trumpet that sings of fame.

"Not as the flying come,
  In silence and in fear,
  They shook the depths of the desert gloom
  With their hymns of lofty cheer.

"Amid the storm they sang,
  And the stars heard and the sea;
  And the waiting isles of promise rang
  With the anthems of the free.

"The ocean eagle soared
  From his nest by the white wave's foam;
  And the rocking pines of the forest roared,
  This is your welcome home.

"What sought they thus afar?
  Bright jewels of the mine?
  The wealth of seas, the spoils of war?
  They sought a faith's pure shrine.

"All, call it holy ground,
  The spot where first they trod:
  They've left unstained what there they found,
  Freedom to worship God."

To review the history of our great nation is but to trace the wonderful providence of God. Look at the very men who directed and guarded the infancy of our republic; whether in the cabinet, or in the camp, whether in the national council or on foreign diplomacy, "their like we shall never see again." **For this very end they seemed to have been born; and they evidently believed in their Divine destination.**

There was a time when darkness shrouded the breath of heaven; not one gleam of light nor a solitary star was seen struggling through the dim distance. Congress paused under the dreadful gloom, when it was agreed to submit their cause to the arbitration of Heaven. A day of solemn fasting and prayer was proposed; instantly the resolution passed with deep emotion. The council-chamber was closed; grave senators retired in silence, personally to engage in fervent prayer; holy ministers of God at the altar, and pious women, with their babies pressed to their bosoms, lifted their streaming eyes to heaven; while Washington was on his knees, when *"a nation was born at once"* – born on the 4th day of July, 1776.

Preserved as *"an handful of corn scattered on the summit of the mountains, a little one has become a thousand, and a small one a strong nation." "It is the Lord's doings, and marvelous in our eyes;"* for according to his promise, *"the Lord has hastened it in his time."*

O happy America! O favored children of the free! when will the great heart of thy mighty people fully know God and the salvation of his Son! "Then Gentiles and kings shall see thy glory, and thou shalt be called by a new name, which the mouth of the Lord shall name. Thou shalt no more be termed Forsaken: neither shall thy land any more be termed Desolate: but thou shalt be called Hephzibah, and thy land Beulah: for the Lord delighteth in thee." Then shall thy glory continue; for *"Thy sun shall no more go down, neither shall thy moon withdraw itself; for the Lord shall be thine everlasting light, and the days of thy mourning shall be ended."*

Excerpts from

Our Great Seal

by E. Raymond Capt

Whenever God has a place in His providence for a man or a nation we would expect to find such mentioned in Bible prophecy. Rev. F. E. Pitts of Nashville, Tennessee in his address to the Congress of the United States in 1857 (recorded in the Congressional Records) spoke the following words:

> *"There are very many passages of Scripture which are universally admitted, by the learned and judicious, to foretell the rise of a great nationality in the latter times. These predictions cannot, by any reasonable construction be applied to the rise of such nationality in the land of Judea; but are most wonderfully descriptive of the United States of America, and of no other country under heaven."*

There is a short chapter in Isaiah which means nothing to any commentator, preacher or layman unless he has discovered that the Prophet Isaiah was given a vision of *America* as existing and playing a conspicuous part in the providence of God among the nations of the earth. The text is in that part of Isaiah where "the burden" of the various nations is given, or, as the margin gives it: "The Oracle concerning Babylon which Isaiah, the son of Amos, did see concerning Moab, concerning Damascus, concerning Egypt, concerning the wilderness of the sea, of those nations of northern Europe where they have to dike out the water in order to till the land, concerning the valley of vision which is Palestine and concerning Tyre." Right in the midst of these whose future is definitely prophesied; enclosed in a circle of the then known nations, a country and a people are described and prophesied that are not named.

This chapter 18 is admittedly a most difficult passage for the interpreter. It is one of the most obscure prophecies; the people to whom it is addressed, the person he sends, the ambassadors, the nations to whom they are sent are extremely doubtful. Most commentators pass it by with brief and inane words showing they have no idea of its meaning. In such translations you may look for poor work in rendering the meaning of unknown words. In this respect, chapter 18 of Isaiah is one of the most inaccurate, awkward and indefinte translations of the Old Testament.

The Hebrew word "hoi erets" with which chapter 18 opens is a mistranslation. It is not an exclamation of "woe," but hailing for atttention, i.e., "Ho" or "All hail." It is the same word used in the same sense in the 55th chapter of Isaiah, "Ho, everyone that thirsteth" and the whole tenor of chapter 18 shows that it should be translated in the same manner there. The nation described is not one that is "meted out and trodden down." The tense is wrong. It is more accurately translated "That meteth out and treadeth down." It is not "scattered and peeled" or "spread out and polished" but "tall and smooth." Its land and rivers have not "spoiled" or "divided" but "quartered."

ISAIAH'S VISION OF OUR COUNTRY

Chapter 18

1 – *Woe to the land shadowing with wings, which is beyond the rivers of Ethiopia:*

2 – *That sendeth ambassadors by the sea, even in vessels of bulrushes upon the waters, saying, Go, ye swift*

messengers, to a nation scattered and peeled, to a people terrible from their beginning hitherto; a nation meted out and trodden down, whose land the rivers have spoiled!*

3 – *All ye inhabitants of the world, and dwellers on the earth, see ye, when he lifteth up an ensign on the mountains; and when he bloweth a trumpet, hear ye.*

4 – *For so the Lord said unto me, I will take my rest, and I will consider in my dwelling place, like a clear heat upon the herbs, and like a cloud of dew in the heat of harvest.*

5 – *For afore the harvest, when the bud is perfect, and the sour grape is ripening in the flower, he shall both cut off the sprigs with pruning hooks and take away and cut down the branches.*

6 – *They shall be left together unto the fowls of the mountains, and to the beasts of the earth: and the fowls shall summer upon them, and all the beasts of the earth shall winter upon them.*

7 – *In that time shall the present be brought unto the Lord of hosts of a people scattered and peeled, and from a people terrible from their beginning hitherto; a nation meted out and trodden under foot, whose land the rivers have spoiled, to the place of the name of the Lord of hosts, the mount Zion.*

Let us give attention to the specific points of description and see if Isaiah does not clearly designate America and the government of the United States.

ONE: *"Woe to the land shadowing with wings, which is beyond the rivers of Ethiopia:"*

In this first verse of Isaiah 18 we find two words which identify the land in question. Since the chapter is not addressed to any land by name, while the other chapters in the Book are specifically addressed, we can conclude the land in question to be a land unknown to Isaiah's time and general territory. This land will be *"beyond the rivers of Ethiopia."* The "rivers" referred to would be the Nile and its tributaries. However, the word "beyond" in Hebrew means "west." When we look today at a map, the top is north, the bottom south, the right is east, and the left is in the west. – Not so in biblical times. The Hebrews faced the sunrise. They looked eastward. "Before" meant east; "behind" or "beyond" meant west; his right arm pointed south and his left to the north. "Beyond" the rivers of Ethiopia (land of Cush) meant over his shoulder *west*. Let Isaiah stand in Jerusalem, face the sunrise and describe the land beyond (west) the rivers of Ethiopia. Following that line of latitude from Jerusalem, west, you will see no country till you strike America at the coasts of South Carolina and Georgia.

The second identification, found in the first verse of Isaiah 18, is the expression *"shadowing with wings,"* which may be rendered "over-shadowing wings" or "outstretched" (wings). Several inferences can be drawn from this expression:

1. It referred to the geographical conformation of the new continent; for a large map of North and South America very much resembles the expanded wings of a great eagle.

2. It is suggestive of the fact that it was a country shadowed or concealed till God was ready for its discovery.

3. It foretold the "spread eagle," the symbol of Americanism. While other countries have the eagle as their national emblem, no other country has the eagle with outstretched wings. Mexico has an eagle with closed wings; Germany has an eagle with closed wings; Russia has an eagle grasping a round globe – representing the whole earth – and an arrow to conquer the earth with war. The United States has an eagle with spread wings and, therefore, it is actually a "land of outstretched wings."

It was Divine Providence that the bald eagle was selected as the emblem of the United States (as a nation), and there is a deep truth hidden under this symbol that is

Scripturally applicable to Israel's deliverance and ultimate repentance. *"And to the woman* [Israel] *were given two wings of the great eagle, that she might fly into the wilderness, unto her place where she is nourished . . ."* (Rev. 12:14)

The prophet Micah describes the idolatry of Israel and the incurable wound of Judah, but speaks of a time when *"Yet will I bring an heir unto thee, O inhabitant of Mareshah; he shall come unto Adullam* [resting place] *the glory of Israel. Make thee bald* [repent], *and poll thee for thy delicate children; enlarge thy baldness* [baldness is the symbol for repentance] *as the eagle; for they are gone into captivity from thee."* (Micah 1:15,16)

The outstretched wings, like a mother bird protecting her brood under her wings, also foreshadowed a nation that would serve as a refuge for all oppressed people of the earth. Since the world began there has never been any country, except America, that from its beginning offered a welcome and hospitality to the downtrodden and suffering people of every part of the world for the purpose of giving them religious freedom and civil liberty.

TWO: *"That sendeth ambassadors by the sea, even in vessels of bulrushes upon the waters . . . ."*

Two points need to be noted here. First, the ambassadors are sent "by sea." The word "ambassadors" means men who travel on business for the government, not those who travel for pleasure or profit. For over 150 years all our ambassadors went by water to Europe, Asia, Australia, even to South and Central America. Only in two countries, Canada and Mexico, did our representatives not have to cross the sea to arrive at their assignments.

Second, when the translators of the King James Version (1611) came to a Hebrew compound word, "water-drinking vessels," they had no idea what it meant, so they looked around for something that grew out of the water and guessed "bulrushes, cattails, flags, papyrus"; hence the words, "vessels of bulrushes." There were Hebrew words for each of those plants, but none were used or meant. However, "vessels that drink" is a perfect description of our modern-day steamship, which was not even dreamed of in Isaiah's time or perceived by the King James translators. But the words *"water drinking vessels upon the waters"* are a picture of the ocean liners, pumping up water, distilling it, turning it into steam to propel its crew, passengers and cargo unto all lands. Isaiah was looking down the ages and seeing the time when America would be exercising a controlling power throughout the world by sending all its ambassadors, soldiers and sailors by vessels that "drink up water" and make steam to propel them on all the waters of the world.

THREE: *"Go, ye swift messengers, to a nation scattered and peeled, to a people terrible from their beginning hitherto; . . ."*

The word "scattered" is from the Hebrew "mashak" meaning "drawn out" or "tall." The word "peeled" is from the Hebrew "marat" meaning "to pluck off hair" or "smooth-shaven." It is evident that the prophet had a vision of a land wherein the men were tall like trees with the bark peeled off, and the best translation available is "tall and clean-shaven."

The year 1000 was the first discovery of America by the Norsemen who came over to Canada and Massachusetts from Greenland. They found a race inhabiting this continent, "tall and smooth." The Indians were taller than the Asians or Europeans and were without beards. The description of this land, possessed, originally, by a people *"terrible from their beginning,"* is a true description of the fierce and war-like Indian tribes found in this new world; broken up into numerous tribes, dispersed without order over the whole country and wasted by continual tribal wars.

It is noteworthy that Isaiah's description of a "people tall and smooth" and "terrible from their beginning" not only fits the original inhabitants of America, but its later people as well. In the World War of 1914, America mobilized an army of three million soldiers that averaged five feet, eleven inches in height. This was the tallest army the world had ever seen, and there was not a full beard among them. Convinced they were fighting a "just war," they were a "terror" unto the enemy. Even in the process of being born, our nation whipped the mightiest nation of the known world ("terrible from their beginning") and fought victorious with Mexico, Spain, Germany, and Japan. We have never been defeated in the defense of our own lands or the freedom of the seas. The word "onward" in the prophecy suggests that America will never be conquered from without down to the end of the ages.

FOUR: *". . . a nation meted out and trodden under foot . . ."*

The word *"meteth"* out is from the Hebrew "qav-qav" meaning "line-line." "Treadeth down" (or trodden down – King James) is from the Hebrew "Mebusoh," which may be rendered "trodden under foot." Putting them together, a literal translation would be a land "measured out under the treading" – that is a land measured out by lines under feet. This is descriptive of our process of surveying, which began in 1800 and in which our land became literally a checkerboard of sections. About the time that Florida and Louisiana were taken into the Union and Ohio became a state, the government passed a law that all public lands should be surveyed by the north star, a base line run east and west and all this land marked up into mile square sections. These sections were then subdivided into quarter sections of half mile squares. No nation was ever so "meted" out in blocks before. All the countries of the earth, as in the division of the land under Joshua, surveyed and marked their land by local boundaries.

FIVE: *". . . whose land the rivers have spoiled, . . ."*

The Revised Version translates *"whose land the rivers divide."* However, the word "spoiled" is from the Hebrew "baza" meaning "to cleave," a term used in the ritual of sacrifice where an animal is hung up and divided into four quarters. The word should be rendered, literally, "quartered." An examination of all nations of the world shows only one, the United States, that is quartered by rivers.

The Mississippi River takes its rise near the Canadian border and cuts right down to the Gulf of Mexico dividing our land in half. On the Pacific Coast side is the Columbia River. Follow it upward to its junction with the Snake River; follow that upward into close proximity with the source of the Missouri River, which starts in Montana and meanders eastward into the Mississippi, dividing the west in half. On the Atlantic Coast side, begin with the Ohio River and follow it eastward to Pittsburgh and its junction with the Monongahela River that runs by McKeesport. Then follow eastward the Younghiopheny River where at Glenco, Pennsylvania, it becomes the Castleman River. Go on up stream till Wills Creek branches off and takes its source where the Potomac begins and runs to the Bay and the Atlantic, and you have the eastern part of the nation divided in half. Thus the whole land is "quartered by rivers." One cannot find any other land on earth divided in this way, into four sections: Northeast, Northwest, Southeast, Southwest, by rivers.

SIX: *"All ye inhabitants of the world, and dwellers on the earth, see ye, when he lifteth up an ensign on the mountains; and when he bloweth a trumpet, hear ye."*

In this prophetic third verse we find use of the words "ensign" and "trumpet," which are symbols of war. Isaiah saw America lift up its ensign on the mountain (nation) and blow the trumpet – a declaration of war. Twice when America has "declared" war, most of the nations of the world "took heed" and became involved. In each case our nation took leadership in making the terms and the regulations for managing and adjusting the varied claims of the nations.

SEVEN: *"For so the Lord said unto me, I will take my rest, and I will consider in my dwelling place like a clear heat upon herbs, and like a cloud of dew in the heat of harvest."*

"For afore the harvest, when the bud is perfect, and the sour grape is ripening in the flower, he shall both cut off the sprigs with pruning hooks, and take away and cut down the branches."

"They shall be left together unto the fowls of the mountains, and to the beasts of the earth: and the fowls shall summer upon them, and all the beasts of the earth shall winter upon them."

These words of Isaiah 18:4-6 are so highly figurative (Eastern) that it is difficult for the Western mind to understand their meaning. A possible interpretation is that the Prophet is speaking of a nation blessed with fertile soil, sunshine and showers (clouds of dew) favorable for cultivation and bountiful harvest, and natural resources favorable to national productivity. But in verse 5, branches of ill omen (*"sprigs"*) will spring up with the luxurious prosperity that comes to the country.

However, a time of cleansing (for our nation) is indicated as "afore the harvest." Matt. 13:39 tells us that the harvest is the consummation of the age. So, at the close of the age, those worthless evil branches are to be pulled off and exposed, and left for the predatory external forces, here called "fowls" and "beasts" to destroy.

EIGHT: *"In that time shall the present be brought unto the Lord of hosts of a people scattered and peeled, and from a people terrible from their beginning hitherto; a nation meted out and trodden under foot, whose land the rivers have spoiled, to the place of the name of the Lord of hosts, the mount Zion."*

In this closing verse we are shown the outcome of the cleansing. As in the parable of the wheat and the tares, the removal of the wicked forces is shown to precede the time that the people turn to God. Also in verse 7, we find that this Christian land, the "place of the name of the Lord of hosts," bears one name in the passage, the name of "the mount Zion."

Beginning with the 40th chapter of Isaiah, we again find prophecies concerning America-Israel. Chapter 40 is an acknowledgment that God is keeping an eye on our forefathers, according to His covenant, although they had been scattered into far distant countries: to the West, to the

East, to the North and to the South (Gen. 28:14). The essence of the chapter is expressed in the lines: *"Comfort ye, comfort ye, my people, saith your God . . . Have ye not known? Have ye not heard? Hath it not been told you from the beginning? . . . It is he that sitteth upon the circle of the earth."* This text was the theme of Handel's wonderful oratoria, "The Messiah," which would mean a great deal more to the listeners if they recognized that its comforting stanzas are actually addressed to Israel's race.

If one studies carefully Isaiah's words, he will discover that God is speaking to Israel in New Testament times, far away from Old Palestine. From the 41st chapter onward, God addresses His people in the "appointed place," in the Islands of the West and in America: *"Keep silence before me, O islands; and let the people renew their strength; let them come near, then let them speak: let us come near together to judgment. Who raised up the righteous man from the east, called him to his foot, gave the nations before him, and made him rule over kings? He gave them as the dust to his sword, and as driven stubble to his bow . . . But thou, Israel, art my servant, Jacob, whom I have chosen, the seed of Abraham my friend . . . Fear not, thou worm Jacob, and ye men of Israel; I will help thee, saith the Lord, and thy redeemer, the Holy One of Israel."*

In the 42nd chapter of Isaiah, God asks the question: *"Who is blind but my servant?"* Yet He is pleased for His righteousness sake: *"Behold my servant, whom I uphold; mine elect, in whom my soul delighteth; I have put my spirit upon him: he shall bring forth judgment to the Gentiles* [nations] . . . *I the Lord have called thee in righteousness, and will hold thine hand, and will keep thee, and give thee for a covenant of the people, for a light of the Gentiles; To open the blind eyes, to bring out prisoners from the prison, and them that sit in darkness out of the prison house . . . Hear, ye deaf; and look, ye blind, that ye may see. Who is blind, but my servant? or deaf as my messenger that I sent? Who is blind as he that is perfect, and blind as the Lord's servant? Seeing many things, but thou observest not; opening the ears, but he heareth not. The Lord is well pleased for his righteousness' sake; he will magnify the law, and make it honourable."*

In the 43rd chapter we read: *"But now thus saith the Lord that created thee, O Jacob, and he that formed thee O Israel, Fear not: for I have redeemed thee, I have called thee by thy name; thou art mine. When thou passeth through the waters, I will be with thee; and through the rivers, they shall not overflow thee; when thou walkest through the fire, thou shalt not be burned; neither shall the flame kindle upon thee . . . Even every one that is called by my name: for I have created him for my glory, I have formed him; I have made him. Bring forth the blind people that have eyes, and the deaf that have ears . . . Ye are my witnesses, saith the Lord, and my servant whom I have chosen: . . . This people have I formed for myself; they shall shew forth my praise."*

Chapter 49 addresses Israel as having been appointed by God as His steward and witness; to be a servant nation unto Him; to colonize the earth; and be a channel of blessing to all nations of the earth. *"Listen O isles, unto me; and hearken, ye people, from far; . . . Thou art my servant, O Israel, in whom I will be glorified . . . I will also give thee for a light to the Gentiles [nations], that thou mayest be my salvation unto the end of the earth . . . Thus saith the Lord, In an acceptable time have I heard thee, and in a day of salvation have I helped thee: and I will preserve thee, and give thee for a covenant [Brith] of the people, to establish the earth, to cause to inherit the desolate heritages [America]; That thou mayest say to the prisoners, Go forth; to them that are in darkness, Shew yourselves. They shall feed in the ways, and their pastures shall be in all high places . . . Behold I have graven thee upon the palms of my hands; thy walls are continually before me."*

Isaiah makes it clear that God is speaking to the "Lost Tribes of Israel" in these words: *"Thus saith the Lord, Where is the bill of your mother's divorcement, whom I have put away? or which of my creditors is it to whom I have sold you? Behold for your iniquities have ye sold yourselves, and for your transgressions is your mother put away."* (Isaiah 50:1) Israel, Jehovah's wife of the Old Testament, had sold herself, was divorced from Him, and is to be brought under the influence of the New Covenant (accept Christianity).

During the Christian dispensation, Lost Israel was to possess certain "marks" of identification. These God-given marks are very many, and while the following list is not exhaustive, it constitutes a chain of evidence utterly impossible to ignore.

1. **Israel to be a great and mighty nation.**
   Gen. 12:2; 18:18; Deut. 4:7,8.
2. **Israel to have multitudinous seed.**
   Gen. 13:16; 15:5; 22:17; 24:60; 26:4, 24; 28:3, 14; 32:12; 49:22; Isa. 10:22; Hos. 1:10; Zech. 10:7,8.
3. **Israel to spread abroad to the West, East, North and South.**
   Gen. 28:14; Isa. 42:5,6.
4. **Israel to have a new home.**
   II Sam. 7:10; I Chron. 17:9.
5. **Israel's home to be north-west of Palestine.**
   Isa. 49:12; Jer. 3:18.
6. **Israel to live in islands and coasts of the earth.**
   Isa. 41:1; 49:1-3; 51:5; Jer. 31:7-10.
7. **Israel to become a company of nations.**
   Gen. 17:4-6, 15,16; 35:11; 48:19; Eph. 2:12.
8. **Israel to have a Davidic King (a perpetual monarchy within Israel).**
   II Sam. 7:13,19; I Chron. 22:10; II Chron. 13:5; Psa. 89:20,37; Eze. 37:24; Jer. 33:17,21,26.
9. **Israel to colonize and spread abroad.**
   Gen. 28:14; 49:22; Deut. 32:8; 33:17; Psa. 2:8; Isa. 26:15; 27:6; 54:2; Zech. 10:8,9.
10. **Israel to colonize the desolate place of the earth.**
    Isa. 35:1; 43:19,20; 49:8; 54:3; 58:11,12.
11. **Israel to lose a colony, then expand, demanding more room.**
    Isa. 49:19,20.
12. **Israel to have all the land needed.**
    Deut. 32:8.
13. **Israel to be the first among the nations.**
    Gen. 27:29; 28:13; Jer. 31:7.

14. Israel to continue as a nation for ever.
    II Sam. 7:16, 24,29; I Chron. 17:22-27; Jer. 31:35-37.

15. Israel's home to be invincible by outside forces.
    II Sam. 7:10; Isa. 41:11-14.

16. Israel to be undefeatable – defended by God.
    Num. 24:8,9; Isa. 15-17; Micah 5:8,9.

17. Israel to be God's instruments in destroying evil.
    Jer. 51:20; 51:19-24; Dan. 2:34,35.

18. Israel to have a land of great mineral wealth.
    Gen. 49:25,26; Deut. 8:9; 33:15-19.

19. Israel to have a land of great agricultural wealth.
    Gen. 27:28; Deut. 8:7,9; 28:11; 33:13,14,28.

20. Israel to be rich by trading.
    Isa. 60:5-11; 61:6.

21. Israel to be envied and feared by all nations.
    Deut. 2:25; 4:8; 28:10; Isa. 43:4; 60:10,12; Micah 7:16,17;
    Jer. 33:9.

22. Israel to lend to other nations, borrowing of none.
    Deut. 15:6; 28:12.

23. Israel to have a new name.
    Isa. 62:2; 65:15; Hos. 2:17.

24. Israel to have a new language.
    Isa. 28:11 (The Bible, by means of which God speaks now to Israel,
    is English not Hebrew.)

25. Israel to possess the gates of his enemies.
    Gen. 22:17.

26. Israel to find the aborigines diminishing before her.
    Deut. 33:17; Isa. 60:12; Jer. 31:7-10.

27. Israel to have control of the seas.
    Deut. 33:19; Num. 24:7; Psa. 89:25; Isa. 60:5 (F. Fenton translates
    this last, "when rolls up to you all the wealth of the sea." That
    could not be unless Israel controlled it.)

28. Israel to have a new religion (New Covenant).
    Heb. 8:10-13; 9:17; Matt. 10:5-7; Luke 1:77; 2:32; 22:20;
    John 11:49-52; Gal. 3:13.

29. Israel to lose all trace of her lineage.
    Isa. 42:16-19; Hos. 1:9,10; 2:6; Rom. 11:25.

30. Israel to keep Sabbath for ever (one day in seven set aside).
    Ex. 31:13,16,17; Isa. 58:13,14.

31. Israel to be called the sons of God (i.e., accept Christianity).
     Hos. 1:10-11.

32. Israel to be a people saved by the Lord.
     Deut. 33:27-29; Isa. 41:8-14; 43:1-8; 44:1-3; 49:25,26; 52:1-12;
     55:3-10,13; Jer. 46:27,28; Eze. 34:10-16; Hos. 2:23; 13:9-14;
     14:4,6.

33. Israel to be the custodians of the Oracles (Scriptures) of God.
     Psa. 147:19,21; Isa. 59:21.

34. Israel to carry the Gospel to all the world.
     Gen. 28:14; Isa. 43:10-12 (witnesses), 21; Micah 5:7.

35. Israel to be kind to the poor and set slaves free.
     Deut. 15:7,11; Psa. 72:4; Isa. 42:7; 49:9; 58:6.

36. Israel to be the heir of the world.
     Rom 4:13.

37. Israel to be God's Glory.
     Isa. 46:13; 49:3; 60:1,2.

38. Israel to possess God's Holy Spirit as well as His Word.
     Isa. 44:3; 59:21; Hag. 2:5.

39. Israel to be God's Heritage, formed by God, for ever.
     Deut. 4:20; 7:6; 14:2; II Sam. 7:23; I Kings 8:51,53; Isa. 43:21;
     54:5-10; Hos. 2:19,23; Joel 2:27; Micah 7:14-18.

40. Israel is the nation appointed to bring glory to God.
     Isa. 41:8-16; 43:10,21; 44:23; 49:3.

These are but a few of the "marks," or "signs," God
has given in His Word by which we may know and recognize
His lost people. None of the nations of the earth respond to
all these identifications except the Anglo-Saxon-Celtic and
kindred peoples under the leadership of the United States of
America (Manasseh) and Great Britain (Ephraim). Joseph (the
birthright nation) was the recipient of all the preceding marks.
By inheritance, his two sons, Ephraim and Manasseh are
found possessing them all. While Israelites remain in other
countries, many came in separate migrations to America as
Britains, Germans, Scandinavians and other national names.
Thus America (one out of many) is representative of the
whole House of Jacob.

AMERICA'S DESTINY

The belief that America has been providentially chosen for a special destiny has roots in the American past. It is by no means a belief that has been given up in this secular age. Such a belief is the focus of American sacred ceremonies, the inaugural addresses of our presidents and the sacred Scriptures of the civil religion. This American destiny, under God, is at the heart of the attempt by contemporary Americans to understand their nation's responsibility at home and abroad. Our responsibility in these matters is deepened because our forefathers (Israel) were the people with whom God made His unalterable Covenant.

The concept of a "chosen nation" is found in the Bible in the narration of the events occuring at the Red Sea when the Hebrew people were saved from the wrath of the Egyptians: *"For thou art an holy people unto the Lord thy God: the Lord thy God hath chosen thee to be a special people unto himself, above all people that are upon the face of the earth. The Lord did not set his love upon you, nor choose you, because ye were more in number than any people; for ye were the fewest of all people: But because the Lord loveth you, and because he would keep the oath which he had sworn unto your fathers, hath the Lord brought you out with a mighty hand and redeemed you out of the house of bondmen, from the hand of Pharaoh king of Egypt."* (Deut. 7:6-8)

The early Pilgrims came to America with the biblical awareness of God guiding them to an "appointed" land where they would form a nation with a divine mission to the whole world. Governor John Winthrop stated it clearly in 1630: "The God of Israel is among us . . . We shall be as a city upon a hill." This idea influenced public opinion in the eighteenth century and continues to be a part of America's self-image today.

The landing of our Pilgrim forefathers on Plymouth Rock, November 21, 1620, was no mere accident. This was Joseph's land, and of it the patriarch Jacob spoke when he said: *"Joseph is a fruitful bough, even a fruitful bough by a well; whose branches run over the wall."* (Gen. 49:22) When the Pilgrims established their first colonies on this shore they found it a great wilderness, and it is spoken of in many places as "the wilderness." In the Book of Revelation, we find Israel fleeing into the wilderness to a place prepared by God: a place where Israel would dwell in safety. Also we find the following verse concerning Israel's sojourn in the writings of Hosea: *"Therefore, behold, I will allure her, and bring her into the wilderness and speak comfortably unto her."* (Hosea 2:14)

We do not know how many of the Founding Fathers considered the possibility that some of the post-biblical nations were descendants of the exiled nations of Israel, but many of them were obviously caught up with the idea. This idea, especially strong in New England, appeared in many sermons in the eighteenth century:

"Congress put at the head of this spirited army the only man (Washington) on whom the eyes of all *Israel* were placed. Posterity, I apprehend, and the world itself, inconsiderate and incredulous as they may be of the dominion of Heaven, will yet do so much justice to the divine moral government as to acknowledge that this American *Joshua* was raised up by God, and divinely formed, by a peculiar influence of the Sovereign of the universe, for the great work of leading the armies of this American *Joseph* (now separated from his brethren), and conducting this people through the severe, the arduous conflict, to liberty and independence.

"Already does the new constellation of the United States begin to realize this glory. It has already risen to an acknowledged sovereignty among the republics and kingdoms of the world. And we have reason to hope, and, I believe, to expect, that God has still greater blessings in store for this *vine* which his own right hand hath planted, to make us high among the nations in praise, and in name, and in honor." (Rev. Ezra Stiles, 1783) The "vine" Stiles referred to (planted by God) is of the vineyard of which Isaiah wrote: *"For the vineyard of the Lord of Hosts is the house of Israel."*

Samuel Langdon, a New England Congregational minister (and president of Harvard from 1774 until 1780), in urging the ratification of the federal Constitution, preached a sermon titled, "The Republic of the Israelites An Example to the American States." In his sermon, Langdon detailed evidences of God's providence in the events of American history and prescribed ways to "make a wise improvement" of what God had granted to *"New Israel."*

Langdom goes on to recommend the laws of Moses for the law of the land, and explains the separation and yet interdependence of the moral laws of the Bible upon the civil laws of the state. He also compares the 12 tribes of Israel to the 13 colonies of the United States. (We have shown previously Israel was also divided into 13 hereditary tribes, because Joseph's share was equally given to his two sons, Ephraim and Manasseh – Joshua 14:4).

Rev. Nicholar Street, in a sermon preached at East Haven, Connecticut (April 1777) drew on similarities between biblical Israel and America Israel. Britain was compared to "Egypt" and characters in the Bible were given contemporary counterparts. America is likened to the wilderness the Israelites found themselves in after being "led out of the land of Egypt by the hand of Moses." Street describes Israel's trials and hardships in the wilderness: "We see that God kept the children of Israel in the wilderness for many years after he had delivered them from the hand of Pharaoh, on the account of their wickedness. He led them so long in the wilderness to humble and prove them . . . and one trial after another . . . so our trials in this wilderness state are bringing out our corruptions . . . pride . . . selfishness . . . covetousness . . . ingratitude . . . rebellion . . . impatience . . .

distrust of God and his providence. All these come flowing forth from the midst of us under our trials in as conspicuous a manner as they did from the children of Israel in the wilderness."

Lyman Beecher (father of Harriet Beecher Stowe, authoress of *Uncle Tom's Cabin*), famed New England clergyman and first president of Lane Theological Seminary (1832) in a speech titled "A Plea for the West," declared that the United States was "destined to lead the way of moral and political emancipation of the world . . . it is time she understood her high calling, and was harnessed for the work" and that many of the resources for that destiny lay in the West.

America's Founding Fathers spoke deliberately and persistently of America-Israel's destiny. Thomas Jefferson concluded his second inaugural address with these words: "I shall need . . . the favor of that Being in whose hands we are, who led our fathers, as Israel of old, from their native land and planted them in a country flowing with all the necessaries and comforts of life." According to Jefferson, America was to act as a model democratic Republic, thereby serving as "the world's best hope."

"I always consider the settlement of America with reverence and wonder, as the opening of a grand scene and design in Providence for the illumination of the ignorant, and the emancipation of the slavish part of mankind all over the earth." (A Dissertation on the Canon and Feudal Law – John Adams)

"No people can be bound to acknowledge and adore the invisible hand which conducts the Affairs of men more than the People of the United States. Every step, by which they have advanced to the character of an independent nation, seems to have been distinguished by some token of providential agency." (George Washington)

"The world has its eye upon America. The noble struggle we have made in the cause of liberty has occasioned a kind of revolution in the human segment. The influence of our example has penetrated the gloomy regions of despotism, and has pointed the way to enquiries which may shake it to its deepest foundations." (Alexander Hamilton)

Benjamin Franklin and many other men who founded our nation believed that God was intimately involved in the events of American history, and that "Divine Providence" was the force that moved the United States to liberty and eventually to direct the world to the same end.

Although our Founding Fathers did believe that America had been providentially chosen for a special destiny, they were deeply divided over the meaning of their national mission. The two basic versions of the chosen theme when applied to the relationship between America and the peoples of other countries are:

One: We are to be a "light to the nations," which by force of example will positively influence other peoples and perhaps draw them to an American haven of freedom. This view of American destiny had its classic expression during the Revolution and the Constitutional period, but it had been nursed by the Puritans of Massachusetts Bay and has appeared repeatedly in the course of American history.

Two: We are to actively win others to American principles and to safeguard those principles around the world. This assumption undergirded the foreign-mission enterprises of the American churches during the late nineteenth and early twentieth centuries, and has stimulated and vindicated America's participation in foreign wars.

During the Philippine crisis (1900), Albert J. Beveridge, the Junior Senator from Indiana, delivered a Senate speech giving his views of American destiny. In his conclusion Beveridge asserted that "God marked the American people as His chosen nation to finally lead in the regeneration of the world . . . For God's hand was in it all. His plans were working out their glorious results . . . This is a destiny neither vague nor undesirable. It is definite, splendid and holy." (Congressional Record XXXIII - 1900)

One could go on and on quoting famous men in America's history that mysteriously suggest our descent from Israel of old, and that America has a predestination. The cynic may dispute this assertion and claim they are just coincidental. But there are too many "coincidences" in our history that prove the existence of a prearranged plan on the part of God Almighty, indicating that He is guiding the Destiny of America.

The United States of America is a land of peaceful dwelling places. Within our borders men and women have been able to live in security, free from the foreign invasions that have swept over other lands from time to time throughout the years of our existence. Our national history has exemplified the Lord's appraisal that *"when a strong man armed keepeth his palace, his goods are in peace."* (Luke 11:21) But in our prosperity we have forgotten God and His warning that if we turn aside from the righteousness of His laws, we will no longer be blessed in our undertakings. Christianity has fallen into disfavor.

We have allowed the murky self-indulgency of psychology to replace the Ten Commandments and the Sermon on the Mount. As we traveled this road, from the light into the dark, our vision grew blurred and dim so that we no longer clearly see the Christian way to serve our country and fulfill our mission to the world. In fact, we have come to a time when many people in the United States suggest that it is unconstitutional or undesirable to associate Almighty God with the political and governmental structure of our country.

The liberal in our midst has risen high above us, occupying seats of authority and issuing edicts of regimentation, with the result that the former era of prosperity is ending; freedom is being curtailed and personal liberty destroyed. Our constitutional right to own private arms is being infringed upon. Our children are being used as pawns in socialistic programs. Expressions of patriotism (displaying banners such as "God Bless America," singing patriotic songs, even pledging allegiance to the flag) are discouraged, if not prohibited, in some public schools in America. The grossest immorality is taught by some professors and when exposed is defended under the right of "academic freedom."

Our cities are hot-beds of crime and political graft. Our newsstands are full of filthy and indecent literature. The use of drugs has run rampant, and the use of alcohol is threatening to do likewise. Our courts of justice judge men by a double standard. We say, "This man who steals is honest, but this man who steals is a thief;" or, "These men are innocent until proven guilty, but these men are guilty until proven innocent." We watch in silence while self-serving accusations are treated with respect, but denials by the accused are treated with scorn. The "rights" of the criminals supersede the welfare of the victim. Killers are turned loose to kill again.

The very lifeblood of enterprise that formerly coursed freely through the veins of our economy, enabling men to provide wealth in abundance from forest, hill and mountain, is now being materially restricted. From the much that is now being accomplished by our labors, the taxgatherer leaves us but little. Under our present system of taxation and interest we penalize the industrious and reward the shiftless; confiscate the property of the unfortunate and make them subjects of charity, and then consider ourselves benevolent.

Without exception all the prophets proclaim that the present age will end in turmoil and violence as the result of evil having come to fruition. This is becoming more evident day by day as violent men and aggressive nations move to bring their evil plans to realization. During this time of trouble the prophets of the Lord have declared that the very heaven and earth are to be shaken, for it is the day of God's fierce anger. God says: *"Yet once more I shake not the earth only, but also heaven. And this word, Yet once more, signifieth the removing of those thinigs that are shaken, as of things that are made, that those things which cannot be shaken may remain."* (Heb. 12:26,27)

Jeremiah likens this coming world conflict, which will bring the age to a close, to the destructiveness of a whirlwind: *"Behold, the whirlwind of the Lord goeth forth with fury, a continuing whirlwind: it shall fall with pain upon the head of the wicked. The fierce anger of the Lord shall not return, until he have done it, and until he have performed the intents of his heart: in the latter days ye shall consider it."* (Jer. 30:23,24)

We now live in the latter days, and it is the time of His fury. But the Prophet also declared: *"At the same time, saith the Lord, will I be the God of all the families of Israel, and they shall be my people."* (Jer. 31:1) So protection from the devastating tempest is promised Israel. However, this protection will only come when America understands and assumes her national responsibility before God to confess her transgressions against the laws of God and re-institute those laws as the laws of the land.

Through the centuries, Israel has usually had to be chastised into repentance. Just as God used the Assyrians to chastise Israel, He is building up our enemies to bring us into national repentance. Ezekiel, in Chapter 38, writes of the day when the forces of Gog (anti-christ) gather against Israel (America) saying: *"I will go up to the land of unwalled villages; I will go to them that are at rest, that dwell safely, all of them dwelling without walls, and having neither bars nor gates. To take spoil, and to take a prey; to turn thine hand upon the desolate places that are now inhabited and upon the people that are gathered out of the nations, which have gotten cattle and goods, that dwell in the midst of the land."* (Ezek. 38:11,12)

The people of our nation will be driven to their knees by coming events, and if they are to pray the prayer of the Prophet Joel, lined out for them, word for word, they must first acknowledge that they are God's servant people. Joel's instructions are: *"Let them say, Spare thy people, O Lord, and give not thine heritage to reproach, that the heathen should rule over them: wherefore should they say among the people, Where is their God"?* (Joel 2:17)

As a people, we are no more worthy than any other people. It may be, that because of our neglect of our "Heritage," we are less worthy than any other people. Nevertheless, we are the descendants of Jacob-Israel, of whom God said: *"Will I be the God of all the families of Israel, and they shall be my people."* (Jer. 31:1) In spite of our unrighteousness and national rejection of God in this day, He will not alter His words: *"Thou art my people, and they shall say, Thou art my God."* (Hosea 2:23) Even in the midst of tribulation and trouble, in the light of this Divine guarantee, we can exclaim with the Psalmist: *"The Lord of hosts is with us; the God of Jacob is our refuge."* (Psalm 46:7)

Through Christ we were redeemed to fulfill His mission of salvation of the world: *"But you are a chosen generation, a royal priesthood, an holy nation, a peculiar people; that ye should shew forth the praises of him who hath called you out of darkness into his marvelous light; Which in time past were not a people, but are now the people of God: which had not obtained mercy, but now have obtained mercy."* (I Peter 2:9-10)

The day must come when America-Israel will give voice to the words spoken through the Prophet Hosea: *"Come and let us return unto the Lord: for he hath torn, and he will heal us; he hath smitten, and he will bind us up."* (Hosea 6:1) We await the day of which the Prophet Isaiah wrote: *"Arise, shine, for thy light is come, and the glory of the Lord is risen upon thee. For behold, the darkness shall cover the earth, and gross darkness the people: but the Lord shall arise upon thee, and his glory shall be seen upon thee . . . for the Lord shall be thine everlasting light, and the days of thy mourning shall be ended."* (Isa. 60:1,2,20)

Let us therefore give ear to the call and *"Arise, shine,"* so that the Glory of the Lord through us will be manifested unto all nations, and that by our example they may understand and know the blessings of righteousness. This is the purpose of the mission of us, His people Israel, and the reason for God having "Chosen" us so that we might show forth His praise:

". . . I will also give thee for a light to the Gentiles [nations],
that thou mayest be my salvation unto the end of the earth."
(Isa. 49:6)

To many persons the true meaning of the name "Israel" is
lost or obscured. The fallacy persists that the Israel people
were chosen by God as an object of *favoritism*. It is easy
to believe that America is God's "New Israel" to support
arrogant self-righteousness. It has been all too easy for some
Americans to convince themselves that they have been chosen
to be a free and powerful people, not because of God's
purpose, but because they deserve election. The blessings of
success, wealth and power are readily taken as signs of their
having merited a special place in history.

Nevertheless, the people of Israel were chosen for
"service" and **"responsibility."** God called Israel to convey
to all mankind the blessings of peace, happiness and true
progress. While performing that service, God guaranteed to
Israel the reward that every faithful servant should receive:
the benevolence and protection of the Master. He placed His
own name upon them, "Israel," meaning "sons ruling with
God," and commanded them not to "take it in vain." That they
did so, and lost their name, is a matter of history. That they
will again carry it – to God's honor and service – is clear from
the Scriptures.

The Prophet Isaiah clearly explains Israel's latter day
special mission to the world: *". . . to undo the heavy burdens,
and to let the oppressed go free, and that ye break every yoke"*
[to free all mankind from all forms of bondage or slavery],
". . . to deal thy bread to the hungry" [eliminate hunger
from the earth], *". . . bring the poor that are cast out to thy
house"* [provide a refuge for those homeless and oppressed].
(Isa. 58:6,7)

The Christian Church and her leaders have failed to
recognize America as God's people Israel, though at the same
time declaring that as Christians they are the sons of the
Living God. This is exactly what Hosea stated would be said

of Israel just previous to the awakening to their identity. *"And it shall come to pass, that in the place where it was said unto them, Ye are not my people, there it shall be said unto them, Ye are the sons of the living God."* (Hosea 1:10)

Ultimately, the "Novus Ordo Seclorum" will dawn as lasting peace will be established, and nations will learn war no more. America will then recognize her place in Bible prophecy and assume Israel's responsibilities, thus fulfilling Israel's Destiny as symbolized in the Great Seal of the United States.

THE STORY OF THE LIBERTY BELL

"Proclaim Liberty Throughout All the Land Unto All the Inhabitants thereof." These words were put on the first Liberty Bell at the suggestion of Mr. Isaac Norris in 1751, who was chairman of the committee which ordered the Bell from London. When the Bell arrived in Philadelphia in 1752 and was rung, it broke at the first stroke of the clapper. The Bell was recast and made heavier. The new Bell hung in the City Hall of Philadelphia most of the time, except when the British threatened that city. It was rung at every important event in the history of the colonies, and after 1776 in the history of our young Republic. It also tolled the death of Chief Justice John Marshall in 1835 and cracked again, never to be heard since.

Why did our Liberty Bell crack twice? Is it possible that it did not ring true and proclaim Liberty to all the inhabitants of America? The following explanation is taken from *America's Appointed Destiny* by Frederick Haberman:

"The famous inscription on it (Liberty Bell) was taken from the 10th verse of the 25th chapter of Leviticus, but it was only a small part of that verse, which reads: *"And ye shall hallow the fiftieth year, and proclaim liberty throughout all the land unto all the inhabitants thereof: it shall be a jubilee unto you; and ye shall return every man unto his possession, and ye shall return every man unto his family."*

The Liberty of which Leviticus, chapter 25, verse 10 speaks was based upon the people of ancient Israel and the people of America-Israel hallowing the fiftieth year as a Jubilee year. To understand what a Jubilee cycle of fifty years is, we must study the whole of the 25th chapter of Leviticus. In that chapter we will find that a Jubilee cycle consists of Seven Sabbatic cycles of seven years each plus one year. Every seventh year Israel was commanded not to plant or harvest but to give the land a rest; and every creditor was commanded by the Lord to make a release:

"At the end of seven years, there shall be a releasing, and this is the kind of releasing. Every possessor of mortgaged land which his neighbor has mortgaged shall release it; he shall have no claim against his neighbor or his brother, because it is a Release by the Ever-Living." (Deut. 15:1,2, Fenton Bible)

"But if your brother becomes poor, and his hand fails among you . . . Take no usury or increase from him, but fear your God, and let your brother live with you. You shall not lend your money to him at usury, and you shall not lend him food at an increase; for I am your Ever-Living God, who brought you from the land of the Mitzeraim [Egypt] to give you the land of Canaan, to be for you from the Ever-Living." (Lev. 25:35-38, Fenton Bible)

That is very strong language and hard teaching, and if our pastors ever heard it they tried to forget about it. They thought they did well enough to make the people keep the Ten Commandments: *"Thou shalt not steal;"* *"Thou shalt not commit adultery;"* *"Thou shalt not covet;"* and all the rest. But to expound that nobody has the right to collect interest or usury on a loan, and that every seventh year all debts and mortgages must be cancelled sounded too Utopian even for our clergy!

Yet the prohibition of interest (which is usury) and the command to release all debts and mortgages every seventh year is as fundamental as the Ten Commandments. Those laws were given to curb and control man's natural tendency to collect more than his share of God's blessings, and to assure a just and equitable distribution of wealth to all inhabitants of the land.

It was upon those Divine laws that the Liberty was based which was to be proclaimed every 50th year: "Proclaim Liberty Throughout All the Land unto All the Inhabitants thereof" – liberty from debts, interest, bonds, and mortgages. But such Liberty the signers of our Declaration of Independence did not have in mind. The Liberty Bell could not ring out such Liberty to the people and therefore became mum.

IN GOD WE TRUST

Upon some of the United States coins there appears the motto, "In God We Trust." This motto was used for the purpose of suggesting to all peoples that the United States is not a "heathen" nation. The motto was first suggested by Rev. M. R. Watkinson of Ridleyville, Pennsylvania, in a letter to Salmon P. Chase, Secretary of the Treasury, dated November 13, 1861.

The letter stated, in part: "One fact touching our currency has hitherto been seriously overlooked. I mean the recognition of the Almighty God in some form in our coins . . . What if our Republic were now shattered beyond reconstruction? Would not the antiquaries of succeeding centuries rightly reason from our past that we were a heathen nation? . . . I have felt our national shame in disowning God as not the least of our present national disaster."

Under the date of November 20, 1861, Secretary Chase addressed the following words in a letter to the Director of the Mint at Philadelphia: "No nation can be strong except in the strength of God, or safe except in His defense. The trust of our people in God should be declared on our national coins. You will cause a device to be prepared without unnecessary delay with a motto expressing in the fewest and tersest words possible this national recognition."

In the course of implementing Secretary Chase's request, it was found that the Act of January 18, 1837 prescribed the mottoes and devices that should be placed upon the coins of the United States, so that nothing could be done without legislation. In December, 1863, the Director of the Mint submitted to Secretary Chase for approval designs for the new 1, 2, and 3-cent pieces, on which it was proposed that one of the following mottoes should appear: "Our country, our God"; "God, our Trust."

Secretary Chase's reply on December 9, 1863 stated: "I approve your mottoes, only that on that (coin) with the

Washington obverse the motto should begin with the word 'our,' so as to read: 'Our God and our country.' And on that with the shield, it should be changed so as to read, 'In God we trust.'" Congress passed the Act of April 22, 1864 that contained provisions for the use of the motto "In God we trust," and it was upon the 2-cent bronze piece that the motto first appeared.

The Act of March 3, 1865 made it lawful for the Director of the Mint, with the approval of the Secretary of the Treasury, to place the motto, "In God we trust" on such coins "as shall admit of the inscription thereon." Under this Act the motto was placed upon the double eagle, eagle, and half eagle, and also upon the dollar, half and quarter dollars in 1866. The Coinage Act of February 12, 1873 reaffirmed the motto to be inscribed on such coins "as shall admit of such motto."

When the double eagle and eagle of new design appeared in 1907, it was soon discovered that the religious motto had been omitted. In response to a general demand, Congress ordered it restored, and the Act of May 18, 1908 made mandatory its appearance upon all coins on which it had heretofore appeared. The motto appears on all gold and silver coins struck since July 1, 1908, with the exception of certain dimes. It was not mandatory upon the cent and five-cent coins but could be placed thereon by the Secretary of the Treasury, or the Director of the Mint with the Secretary's approval.

The Act of July 11, 1955 makes the appearance of the motto, "In God we trust," mandatory upon all coins of the United States. In that same year a constituent asked Representative Charles E. Bennett of Florida why that motto did not appear on all United States money, both coins and currency. After looking into the matter, Bennett introduced a bill requiring that all future issues of coins and currency bear the motto, which was approved by both the House of Representatives and the Senate.

Further official recognition of the motto is found in a joint resolution passed by the House on April 16 and the

Senate on July 23, and became law with the President's approval on July 30, 1965. It read: "Resolved by the Senate and House of Representatives of the United States of America in Congress assembled, That the national motto of the United States is hereby declared to be 'In God we trust.'"

The House Judiciary Committee, which had considered the resolution and reported it favorably to Congress, had recognized that the phrase, "E. Pluribus Unum," had also "received wide usage in the United States," and the joint resolution did not repeal or prohibit its use as a national motto. In essence, "In God we trust" is **the** motto of the United States, while "E. Pluribus Unum" is **a** motto of the United States.

SYMBOLS OF ISRAEL/AMERICA

AMERICA - "Amer"=Heaven, "Rica"=Kingdom (Kingdom of Heaven)

America - A prophetic name meaning "kingdom of heaven." It has been suggested that it is derived from the old Norse word *"Ommerike"* (oh-meh-ric-eh). *Omme* means "ultimate" or "final" and *Rike* means "kingdom." It is a slightly corrupted form of the more ancient Visigothic word *"amalric." Amal* means "heaven" and *ric* means "Kingdom." (Phonetically, the "l" and "r" are interchangeable in many languages, thus giving the word **"amarric"** which needs only the closing breath to be **America**.) The same old word has been handed down today in the modern German word *"Himmelreich"* used in the German New Testament to mean Kingdom of Heaven. Thus **Amalric, Himmelreich** and **America** are synonymous. This name given to our land was no mere accident but in reality is prophetic of the bright age to come.

JERUSALEM - (America, the New Jer**USA**lem)

FLAG - Our flag is made up from the colors of scarlet, blue and white, the colors of Israel of old. These colors covered the table of shew bread within the Tabernacle. **Red,** the color of blood, signified justice or judgment, reminding us of the shed blood of Christ for the redemption of His people Israel: **White,** the color of snow, signified purity or holiness (Psalm 50:7; Isaiah 1:18). **Blue,** the color of the sky, signified love, and because this is the color of the heavens it is representative of God.

THIRTEEN - Thirteen is the number of Israel. There are 13 tribes of Israel. Joseph, one of the twelve sons of Jacob, received a double portion from his father to include his two sons, Ephraim and Manasseh (Gen. 48).

America began with thirteen colonies. This number is significant in American symbols. Our flag has thirteen stripes, and our Great Seal incorporated the number thirteen in many of its heraldic elements.

THE GREAT SEAL

OBVERSE - The front side of the seal is made up of six parts: 1. The Eagle, 2. The Shield, 3. The Scroll, 4. The Motto, 5. The Olive Branch, 6. The Bundle of Arrows.

The Eagle - Our national bird is a symbol for God (Exodus 19:4). It is deserving of the chief place on our coat of arms.

The Shield - It is composed of **thirteen** stripes banded across the top with blue. The thirteen stripes represent the **thirteen** colonies supported by the blue band above signifying dependence upon God (Psalm 5:12).

The Scroll - It is unsealed, rolled out, and its words openly displayed for all to read. The motto is composed of **thirteen** letters, "E Pluribus Unum," (Out of Many, One). Our people have come from many nations, but we are one under God who is the Divine Architect of our nation.

The Olive Branch - It is held in the eagle's right talon and consists of **thirteen** leaves and **thirteen** berries. God likened Israel to an olive tree which stands for peace (Jer. 11:16; Hos. 14:5-7). America has always strived to maintain peaceful relations with other countries. Whenever forced into war with another country, America has never taken spoils. Our history has been to help defeated nations recover.

The Bundle of Arrows - It is held in the eagle's left talon and consists of **thirteen** arrows and **thirteen** feathers. The arrows are pointed upward to represent the military power of the nation, which is always in a state of readiness to maintain freedom in the world. Arrows were the weapons of the Israelites for centuries (2 Chron. 14:8; I Chron. 12:2; I Chron. 5:18).

The Crest - The crest is composed of three main parts: 1. The Glory, 2. The Cloud, 3. The Constellation. The Glory surrounds the crest and denotes the presence of God over, and in the midst of, our nation. The Glory was manifested to the children of Israel in the wilderness as a pillar of fire at night. The Cloud in Scripture denotes the presence of God (Num. 16:42). The cloud guided the Israelites in the wilderness by day (Ex. 13:21). The Constellation is composed of **thirteen** 5-pointed stars in the midst of the Glory Cloud. In scriptural heraldry such a star was a symbol of God's protective care.

REVERSE - This side of the seal consists of six parts: 1. The Unfinished Pyramid, 2. The Mystical Eye, 3. The Radiant Triangle, 4. The Words "Annuit Coeptis," 5. The Motto, "Novus Ordo Seclorum," 6. The Numerical Letters "MDCCLXXVI."

The Unfinished Pyramid - This pyramid, identified with the Great Pyramid of Gizeh (Is. 19:19-20), consists of **thirteen** courses of stone to represent "strength and duration." It is a reminder of our ancestors, the Children of Israel, during their long sojourn in the land of Egypt.

The Mystical Eye - It symbolizes the watchful eye of the God of Israel watching over the destiny of this nation (Ps. 121:4; Jer. 24:6; Ps. 32:8; Deut. 32:10).

The Radiant Triangle - This is the emblem of "God's Eternal Glory." It forms the cap-stone or "corner stone" of the unfinished pyramid. In Scripture, Jesus Christ is symbolized by such a stone (Matt. 21:42; Ps. 118:22; Eph. 2:20-21).

The Motto - Above the Reverse Crest, in **thirteen** letters, is the motto, "Annuit Coeptis," meaning "He hath prospered our undertakings" (or beginnings). This motto refers to God prospering our people who were set apart for a special purpose in the latter days, and whose greatness was prophetically assured.

The Motto - "Novus Ordo Seclorum" means "A mighty Order of Ages is born anew." This new nation would be different from all other nations before it: a government by the people and for the people; a resurrection of the kingdom of Israel with Almighty God as its Creator. Individual liberty and freedom would be the hallmark of this land.

The Date - **MDCCLXXVI** - This date on the base of the pyramid is the date of our independence. It is the beginning of a new nation, the nucleus of the Kingdom of God on earth with all its glorious promises to long oppressed humanity.

Excerpts from Our Great Seal

BATTLE HYMN OF THE REPUBLIC

Mine eyes have seen the glory of the coming of the Lord;
He is tramping out the vintage where the grapes of wrath are stored;
He hath loosed the fateful lightning of His terrible swift sword;
His truth is marching on.

I have seen Him in the watch-fires of a hundred circling camps;
They have builded Him an altar in the evening dews and damps;
I have read His righteous sentence by the dim and flaring lamps;
His day is marching on.

I have read a fiery gospel writ in burnished rows of steel,
"As ye deal with my contemners, so with you my grace shall deal;
Let the Hero, born of woman, crush the serpent with his heel,
Since God is marching on."

He has sounded forth the trumpet that shall never call retreat;
He is sifting out the hearts of men before his judgment-seat;
O, be swift, my soul, to answer Him! be jubilant my feet:
Our God is marching on.

In the beauty of the lilies Christ was born across the sea,
With a glory in His bosom that transfigures you and me;
As He died to make men holy, let us die to make men free,
While God is marching on.

(CHORUS)

Glory, glory, hallelujah!
Glory, glory, hallelujah!
Glory, glory, hallelujah!
His truth is marching on.

Howe

Excerpts from

ABRAHAMIC COVENANT

by E. Raymond Capt

There are those that claim that America is not a "Christian nation" as this would be discriminatory against other religions. However that may be, the records of the group of men that gathered in Philadelphia in 1776 – Washington, Franklin, Jefferson – show they did establish this nation under God (Christ).

Also, America has been legally declared a Christian nation many times by the Supreme Court of the United States. Foremost was the declaration February 29, 1892 in a case involving a church and certain taxes (Holy Trinity Church vs. United States, 143 U.S. 471). The highest court of the land, after mentioning various circumstances, added the following words: *"and these and many other matters which might be noticed, add a volume of unofficial declarations to the mass of organic utterances that this is a* **CHRISTIAN NATION.**"

Let it be noted that this nation is not "anti" any religion, and it is not "hetero-religious" (many religions). It is Christian. It recognizes worship of God through Christ, the Saviour, the only Mediator between God and man. As a Christian nation, it is generous and tolerates freedom of worship. But, as a nation, it is not merely "religious," it is Christian.

It should also be noted that the framers of all the early Constitutions of the States recognized this nation as a Christian nation. This was evidenced by such points as: belief in Christ being a condition of holding public office, tax support and maintenance of public Christian schools, recognition of Sunday as the Lord's Day and recognition of Deity. This was expressed in terms such as *"Grateful to Almighty God," "So help me God"* and *"in the name of God, Amen."* And often reference was made to the God of the Old and New Testaments of the Bible.

The members of the Supreme Court of the United States take their oath of office with their hand on the Bible, the Testimony of Jesus Christ, thus recognizing His authority as being greater than theirs. Washington, when offered a crown to establish this nation as a monarchy, said: *"America already has a King. God is our King."* Who was the King of Israel? God was the King of Israel, and He was the King of no other nation but Israel.

Going back to the establishment of the first colonies we find that in 1606, King James I of England, who issued the first Charter, began with these words: *"We greatly commending, and graciously accepting of, their desires for the furtherance of so noble a work, which may be the providence of Almighty God, hereafter tend to the glory of His Divine Majesty, in propagating the Christian religion to such people as yet live in darkness and miserable ignorance of the true knowledge and worship of God."* Subsequent charters were issued in 1609 and 1611 containing the same religious reference. The Pilgrim Fathers who risked their lives and limbs to cross the sea did so *"for the glory of God and advancement of the Christian faith."*

In 1620, the Pilgrims, in their tiny boat the Mayflower, crossed the broad Atlantic to accomplish the noble words expressed in their now famous compact: *"Having undertaken for the glory of God, and the advancement of the Christian faith, and the honor of our king and country, a voyage to plant the first colony in the northern parts of Virginia."*

And in the same year, King James I, in answer to another petition, granted the New England Charter, in which was included the following clause: *"We according to our princely inclination, favoring much their worthy disposition, in hope thereby to advance the enlargement of the Christian religion, to the glory of God Almighty."* The Charter of Massachusetts Bay granted by King William and Queen Mary, and preceding the one by King Charles I, stated in part: *"may win and incite the natives of the country to their knowledge and obedience of the only true God and Saviour of mankind, and the Christian faith."*

The fundamental orders of Connecticut, under which a provisional government was instituted in 1638-1639 stated: *"and well knowing where a people are gathered together the Word of God requires that to maintain the peace and union of such a people there should be an orderly and decent government established according to God, to order and dispose of the affairs of the people at all seasons as occasion shall require; do therefore associate and conjoin ourselves to be as one public State or Commonwealth, and do, for ourselves and our successors and such as shall be adjoined to us at any time hereafter, enter into combination and confederation together, to maintain and preserve the liberty and purity of the gospel of our Lord Jesus which we now profess . . . Which, according to the truth of said gospel, is now practiced amongst us."*

One could go on and on, showing by history, tradition and statistics that the United States is, in fact, a Christian nation. Christianity came to this country with the first colonist; has ever been powerfully identified with its rapid development, both as a colonial and national government, and today exists as a mighty factor in the life of the Republic of the United States.

In like manner much could be shown by history and tradition that the United States of America is from the tribe of Manasseh, and is peopled by a gathering of all the thirteen tribes of Israel. Our Pilgrim Fathers, who called themselves *"the seed of Abraham, God's servant and the children of Jacob, His chosen,"* allotted their land as Israel did. They followed after the council of Moses, the lawgiver of Israel, and in all their undertakings asked for the guidance and blessings of the God of Jacob, Isaac and Abraham.

The name Manasseh means "forgetfulness" and if there has ever been a people forgetful of all their past, it is this last, this thirteenth, this Manasseh-Israel people in the United

States. However, America, as prophesied of Manasseh, did become the great nation, (Gen. 48:19) ONE OUT OF MANY (E Pluribus Unum), and took her place in the appointed time in fulfillment of God's Covenant with Abraham.

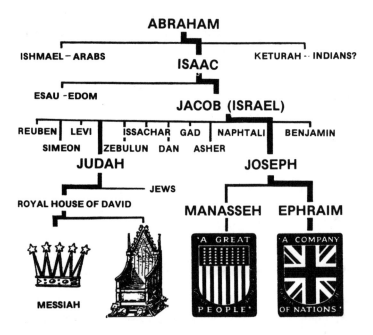

America has yet to recognize her relationship to God, and re-institute His laws. Through the centuries Israel has usually had to be chastised into repentance. Just as God used the Assyrians to chastise Israel, He is building up the enemies of Israel-America to bring them into national repentance. Ezekiel, in chapter 38, writes of the day when the forces of Gog (antichrist) gather against Israel, saying: *"I will go up to the land of unwalled villages; I will go to them that are at rest, that dwell safely, all of them dwelling without walls, and having neither bars nor gates. To take a spoil, and to take a prey; to turn thine hand upon the desolate places that are now inhabited, and upon the people that are gathered out of the nations, which have gotten cattle and goods, that dwell in the midst of the land."* (Eze. 38:11,12)

The people of our nation will be driven to their knees by coming events, and if they are to pray the prayer the Prophet Joel lined out for them, word for word, they must first acknowledge that they are God's servant people. Joel's instructions are: *"Let them say, Spare thy people, O Lord, and give not thine heritage to reproach, that the heathen should rule over them: wherefore should they say among the people, Where is their God"*? (Joel 2:17)

As a people, we are no more worthy than any other people. It may be, that because of our neglect of our HERITAGE, we are less worthy than any people; nevertheless, we are the descendants of Jacob-Israel, of whom God said: *"Will I be the God of all the families of Israel, and they shall be my people."* (Jer. 31:1) In spite of our unrighteousness and national rejection of God, He will not alter His word: *"Thou art my people, and they shall say, thou art my God."* (Hosea 2:23)

The day will come when America-Israel will give voice to the words spoken through the Prophet Hosea: *"Come, and let us return unto the Lord: for he hath torn, and he will heal us; he hath smitten, and he will bind us up."* (Hosea 6:1) Our God, the God of Abraham, Isaac and Jacob, will yet have the salute of our banners and the allegiance of all the people. The kingdoms of this world shall become the Kingdom of our Lord Jesus Christ, the Everlasting Father, for ever and ever.

"BLOW THE TRUMPET IN ZION – TURN UNTO THE LORD YOUR GOD"

"And thou, O tower of the flock, the strong hold of the daughter of Zion, unto thee shall it come, even the first dominion; the kingdom shall come to the daughter of Jerusalem [The United States of America!] . . . *Now also many nations are gathered against thee, that say, Let her be defiled, and let our eye look upon Zion. But they know not the thoughts of the Lord, neither understand they his counsel: for he shall gather them as the sheaves into the floor. Arise and thresh, O daughter of Zion* [USA]: *for I will make thine horn iron, and I will make thy hoofs brass: and thou shalt beat in pieces many people: and I will consecrate their gain unto the Lord, and their substance unto the Lord of the whole earth."* (Micah 4)

THE
BATTLE OF ARMAGEDDON
The World's Last Conflict
Between
Civil and Religious Liberty On the One Side, and
Political and Ecclesiastical Despotism On the Other

Rev. F. E. Pitts

The voice of the prophetic Scriptures frequently and fully announces the warfare of the world. Preparation for ages has anticipated the struggle; while the clangor of its trumpets is almost heard marshaling its millions to the charge.

It is true as destiny, and the gathering storm is rising. In the volume of inspiration it is termed, *"The Battle of God," "The Battle of Armageddon,"* and *"The Battle of that great day of God Almighty."*

It is symbolized by Daniel in the smiting of the monarchical image by the mountain-stone; by the casting down of the thrones before the Ancient of days; by the destruction of the willful king upon the mountains of Israel, when he shall *"plant the tabernacles of his palace between the two seas."* It is Michael and his angels warring with the dragon and his angels; it is the conquest won by the man on a white horse, who was *"crowned with many crowns;"* it is the taking of *"the beast and the false prophet;"* it is the reaping the harvest of the world and the gathering of the vintage of the earth. It is literally described by Ezekiel, when the chief prince of Meshech, Gomer, Tubal, and Magog, with the multitudinous hosts from Persia, Ethiopia, and Libya, invades *"the land of unwalled villages."* It is the immense armament described by Joel when he exclaims, *"Multitudes! Multitudes in the valley of decision!"* It is described by the Saviour to be *"a time of trouble such as never shall be till that day."* It is the *"gathering together of the kings and nations of the earth to the battle of that great day of God Almighty."*

Such, my countrymen, are some of the unquestionable and sublime allusions in the many, very many Divine declarations that announce the grand and terrible catastrophe – declarations that the clearest acumen and most direct philosophy of language must legitimately apply to the rapidly approaching tempest.

Nevertheless, like all other truths of the inspired volume, however overwhelming the sublimity of the theme, no violence is offered to reason, nor unnecessary embargo imposed upon the faith of mortals.

What subject could possibly enlist a world in arms, if it be not the principle of civil and religious liberty? All other questions, however vital and important, are but local in their influence, and the weightiest results must necessarily be sectional. But the principle of popular freedom is capable of universal diffusion, and must ultimately be commensurate with the nations of the earth. It lies at the foundation of our being, and forms the very texture and fabric of human nature: nay, the very law of our great Creator, and every specification growing out of that law, bear directly upon this twofold principle. To love God and our neighbor plainly indicates the foundation of all true order in the governmental codes of the earth.

Freedom to worship God, and equitable reciprocities amongst our fellow-creatures; wherever these first and great commandments are disregarded by the governments on earth, monarchy, absolutism, or anarchy is found to exist; and this form of government being unfriendly to the free worship of the true God, and a usurpation of the prerogatives of a people to govern themselves, always has been, and ever will be, an uncompromising enemy to civil and religious liberty, until it is annihilated from the nations of the earth.

True, both principles are aggressive, and must continue to enlarge their bounds until a final collision must exterminate the one or the other.

The outbreaks in ages past were only occasional or accidental; still, even in those times monarchy always reconnoitered with a sleepless vigilance every demonstration of popular freedom; and the genius of Republicanism has ever been prompt to prove its utter, uncompromising hostility to monarchy. But in those ages the world was too far apart, the knowledge of the nations too limited, and their contact with one another so seldom, that they seemed to live in comparative indifference to one another. But now, since intellectual and moral light is reaching every shore; commerce spreading every where; the formal representatives of all nations at the world's fairs, in London, New York and Paris; since the wonderful discoveries of gold in California and Australia, bringing the nations together; and since the facilities for travel by land and by sea, and the intercommunication of the magnetic telegraph – the world has come into such immediate proximity, the great issue must come off. The hostile forms of government are now clearly defined and well understood; and the two geniuses, like two Caesars, cannot live in the same world together much longer. For if Republicanism be a failure, it will be overthrown; and if Absolutism be offensive to God, and an outrage upon the people, its days are destined to be numbered.

The truth, as announced in the Bible, of the coming conflict, has always been received in the Church, because it is too obvious to be questioned. Both Jews and Christians maintain it as a subject of Divine revelation; but as they have almost invariably misapplied the passages that foretold a great nationality, by referring them to the Jews, it necessarily led them to lay the scene of the last great battle in the land of Palestine. That the scattered Jews would return to Judea, and the nations and kingdoms of the earth would send an armament of millions to crush out a handful of unambitious people, whom the clemency of Christian countries favored in their return – how perfectly ridiculous! Were all the Jews on earth restored to the small territory of Palestine, what temptation or provocation could they offer to arouse the allied armies of earth to invade them?

No, my countrymen, it is not ancient Jewry that will witness this invasion. There is another Israel, the Israel of America, that has given monarchy more disquietude than ancient Israel ever did in all its glory. And here alone monarchy will find a foeman worthy of its steel, and the only nation on the globe that can measure arms with kings.

Twice in the very infancy of our nation's history the proudest empire on the face of the earth had to pay an involuntary obeisance to the chivalry of our army. But now the young eaglet is fully fledged, and cleaves the heights of heaven; it might be indiscreet to provoke the glance of his eye or the thunder of his pinions. So at least we think.

We shall first notice the preparatory movements that will finally marshal the allied hosts to battle:

"And the sixth angel poured out his vial upon the great river Euphrates; and the water thereof was dried up, that the way of the kings of the east might be prepared. And I saw three unclean spirits like frogs come out of the mouth of the dragon, and out of the mouth of the beast, and out of the mouth of the false prophet, for they are the spirits of devils, working miracles, which go forth unto the kings of the earth and of the whole world, to gather them to the battle of that great day of God Almighty . . . And he gathered them together into a place called in the Hebrew tongue Armageddon."

Now, observe, whatever may be the meaning of the sublime events mentioned in the foregoing passage, they must relate to the preparatory measures that bring on the battle of that great day.

Let us, then, examine the quotation by the most reliable rules of interpretation. A *"river"* in the symbolic prophecies, according to the admission of the best commentators, symbolizes a national commotion. Then, *"the great river Euphrates,"* that swept by ancient Babylon, must represent a commotion or revolution among the nations; but this scene is laid under the sixth vial, which is now acknowledged to embrace the beginning of the present century. Well, when was there ever a greater commotion among the nations than the revolutionary unheavings of the people under the genius of the great Napoleon? But *"the waters of that river were dried up."* This was done at the battle of Waterloo. *"That the way of the kings of the east might be prepared."*

During the storm that was raging throughout Europe under Bonaparte, the allied monarchs that were united to overthrow him found it very inconvenient to act in concert; but immediately after Napoleon was banished to a distant island, there was an assemblage of the principal monarchs: Russia, Prussia, Austria, and England. Though the King of England could not be there in person – for the old man was crazy – yet his regent was there, and represented him in that conference, that was called **"The Triple Alliance."** This name may have been given to this conclave of kings from the three principal monarchs in attendance. But this "triple alliance" has a stronger claim to its **three-fold** character from the **three doctrines** asserted, signed and sealed by this convention of sovereigns. There were precisely **three doctrines** or **principles: Absolutism, Church Supremacy**, and **Legitimacy**, or the **Divine right of kings**. How perfectly fulfilled the prophecy!

"And I saw three unclean spirits like frogs come out of the mouth of the dragon, and out of the mouth of the beast, and out of the mouth of the false prophet. These are

the spirits of devils." The three dogmas are here pronounced to be the spirits or doctrines of devils. All doctrines are the doctrines of devils that are opposed by Divine revelation; but Absolutism, Church Supremacy, and Divine rights of kings are opposed by the word of God; consequently, the three doctrines of the "Triple Alliance" are the doctrines of devils, and specifically fulfill the prophecy. *"Which go forth unto the kings of the earth and of the whole world, to gather them together to the battle of that great day of God Almighty."*

These foul principles represented by **unclean frogs** will summon around the thrones of monarchies the dupes of despotism, and enlist and muster into service the countless legions that shall compose that fearful armament. *"And he gathered them together into a place called in the Hebrew tongue 'Armageddon.'"* On that last great battle-field, the doctrines of the Triple Alliance, with the host of their deluded defenders, shall perish forever.

We now notice some of the symbols of that final engagement, the war itself.

"Forasmuch as thou sawest that the stone was cut out of the mountain without hands, and that it brake in pieces the iron, the brass, the clay, the silver, and the gold; the great God hath made known to the king what shall come to pass hereafter: and the dream is certain, and the interpretation thereof sure."

The four great successive monarchies on earth, as seen in the dream of Nebuchadnezzar, we have shown in our former address to be represented by the metals composing the great image. From the first or golden headed kingdom, the whole of monarchy, to its final overthrow, was represented; for after the annihilation of this image, not the smallest principle or fragment should remain. *"Then was the iron, the clay, the brass, the silver, and the gold, broken to pieces together, and became like the chaff of the summer threshing-floors; and the wind carried them away, that no place was found for them."*

But how are we to understand all these great monarchies to be **destroyed at once**, *"broken to pieces together,"* unless we understand that before the image is smitten by the stone, there must be a reconstruction of all the principles and powers, glory and grandeur, weakness and wickedness, embodied in the corporate image, and represented by the different metals. Such an accumulation of all the principles of monarchy, in some colossal giant of autocracy, must appear in huge embodiment: *"the form thereof,"* like its symbol, will be *"terrible."*

Now, as we have plainly proved that the stone or fifth kingdom that destroys the image is a different kind of government altogether from monarchy, and hostile to it, that fifth government must be a great Republic. In truth, as monarchy restored is seen in the image, Israel, or a providential Republic, must be restored also, in order to the destruction of monarchy.

Let those divines attend who suppose that Christianity is *"the stone cut out of the mountain without hands."* Which of the four great empires did Christianity destroy? The truth is, the Assyrian, the Medo-Persian, and the Macedonian kingdoms had passed away long before Christianity was born. And as for Rome, certainly no good Christian would ever dream that the barbarian hordes from the North who overran the Roman Empire were either good or bad Christians.

From this symbol we are clearly taught:

First. That the whole of monarchy, from the Assyrian down to its utter destruction, is represented in the dream.

Second. That a political government, unconnected with, different from, and hostile to monarchy, would providentially arise in the divided age of the Roman Empire.

Third. That this fifth or stone government would destroy the last vestige of monarchy from the face of the earth.

Fourth. That the destruction of monarchy will be effected by military power. The strong language employed to describe the destruction of the metallic image cannot refer to the gentle and inoffensive religion of Christ. The power of moral suasion, by gradual influence, will change the heart and manners of men. But to overthrow at one single blow a vast political organization, combining millions of subjects, the custom of ages, and the wealth of nations, and that, too, by the mild and gentle genius of a religion whose great Author was meek and lowly, and whose kingdom was not of this world, is out of the question. The very terms used to describe the destruction of the Macedonian Empire by the Romans are also employed to show the annihilation of all the empires by the stone. Now, the conquests made by Rome were effected by the prowess of her arms; none will deny this. If, therefore, Rome herself and the balance of the kingdoms are to be destroyed, it must be by military power also.

The destruction effected by this fearful power is complete, for the image is broken and reduced to infinitesimal atoms: it is scattered to the winds, like chaff from the summer's threshing-floors.

As this conflict put a final end to all earthly monarchy, and as all political governments are either autocratic or democratic, and as the fifth government is to *"Become a great mountain and fill the whole world,"* the conclusion is forced upon us that one of the grand missions of the providential Republic of America is the final overthrow of monarchy and the extension of the principles of popular freedom over the whole world.

The vision of Daniel the prophet was a corroboration of the dream of Nebuchadnezzar the king. The four beasts of Daniel answer to the four metals of the image. The ten horns on the head of the fourth beast answer to the ten toes on the feet of the image. The little horn having eyes, that arose on the head of the last beast, and amongst the other horns, symbolized an ecclesiastical connection with the state, and answers to the union of the clay and iron in the feet.

The rise of the Ancient upon a chariot throne symbolizes a pure political government, combining the principles of a confederated republic, such as was the "ancient" form of government given to the Jews, and answers to the stone *"cut out of the mountain without hands."* The casting down of the thrones before the Ancient answers to the smiting of the monarchical image by the stone. The coming of *"one like to the Son of man to the Ancient,"* and the *"dominion given to the people of the saints,"* answer to the stone becoming *"a great mountain and filling the whole earth;"* and both symbolize the universal spread of civil and religious liberty, until the millennial glory of Christ shall cover the earth as the waters cover the seas.

The vision is indeed a sublime one; and the inexpressible grandeur of the scene has inclined most men to suppose that *"the Ancient of days"* was the Almighty Father. But how can this be? For this is evidently a judgment-scene of the doom of monarchy; for this alone, it seems, the judgment did sit and *"the thrones were cast down."* But, *"the Father judgeth no man."* God the Father is in no place in the Scriptures represented by a human form. Besides, the Almighty is not the *"Ancient of days:"* he is the Ancient of eternity. And the term *"days"* is evidently used in this passage to let men understand that the vision refers to time, and its scenes are to be transacted on earth. Nor can the *"Ancient"* refer to the Son of man, for it is written in the vision that *"one like unto the Son of man came to the Ancient"* afterwards.

"And there was war in heaven: Michael and his angels fought against the dragon; and the dragon fought and his angels, and prevailed not; neither was their place found any more in heaven. And the great dragon was cast out." (Revelation 12:7-8)

This passage is another symbolic announcement of the grand conflict. The contending armies, the battle-scene and its results, are respectively mentioned.

"A dragon," being fabulous, is necessarily a symbol; for, although the word has been applied first to one beast and then to another, there is no certainty if it had any identical original. But the tyrants of the ancient kingdoms were called **dragons**: the despots of Egypt in particular were denominated thus. The Scriptures being then their own interpreter, a dragon is the symbol of political despotism.

Now, as the one part is symbolic, the other must be also. Then *"Michael"* is not, in this case, a literal angel, but stands as the representative of a power opposed to autocracy. That power can only be the genius of popular freedom. Perfectly agreeable to this definition is the character drawn of this same Michael in the Book of Daniel. He is there called *"Michael the great prince, that standeth for the children of thy people:"* that is, he is the sovereignty of the people. The term "heaven" in the passage is also symbolic, and means, when used in the Apocalypse, **the place of the Church,** as the term *"earth,"* when employed under the same circumstances, refers to the seat of the old Roman Empire. As for *"war in heaven,"* the place of future blessedness, no dragon or war will ever be known there; for *"there the wicked cease to trouble, and the weary are at rest."*

Then the war which is to take place between Michael and his angels on the one side, and the dragon and his angels on the other, must foretell the final battle that must inevitably occur between civil and religious liberty and its armies and monarchy and its armies, which, according to the prediction, closes with the glorious triumph of the former over the ruin and annihilation of the latter.

"Michael, the great prince that standeth for thy people," must then, in the book of *Revelation*, be

understood as the symbolic embodiment of popular sovereignty. But, my countrymen, if any one man that ever lived on earth is entitled to be called Michael, the great prince that standeth for the people, it is George Washington, the friend of liberty, and the father of his country.

"And I saw heaven opened, and behold a white horse; and he that sat upon him . . . and in righteousness he doth judge and make war. His eyes were as a flame of fire, and on his head were many crowns . . . And I saw the beast, and the kings of the earth, and their armies, gathered together to make war against him that sat on the horse and against his army. And the beast was taken, and with him the false prophet . . . And the remnant were slain with the sword of him that sat upon the horse." (Revelation 19)

From the best annotators of prophecy, the following is the true and legitimate interpretation of the terms employed:

First. A *"horse"* is a symbol of some form of religion; consequently, a "white horse" must represent a pure and divinely authorized religion.

Second. A *"man"* symbolizes a political government.

Third. *"Crowns"* represent sovereignties: *"many crowns upon his head"* – many State sovereignties united in one political union or confederation. When this same symbolic personage appeared as *"the man-child,"* the number of States represented by the stars were twelve, then thirteen; but now, since the infant "is one hundred years old" at the commencement of the great war, he appears on the battle-field, "crowned with many crowns" – many more States in the confederacy than at the beginning.

Then, we behold in this vision of St. John a political government embracing a confederation of many State sovereignties, acknowledging and confiding in one true and divinely sanctioned religion.

That the United States of America answers to this picture, our very national "E PLURIBUS UNUM" declares.

Here again we behold the forces of monarchy mustered to give battle to a free confederated Republic that sanctions the only true religion. *"For the beast, and the kings of the earth, and their armies, gathered together to make war against him that sat upon the horse, and against his army."* The taking of the beast, and the false prophet, and the kings of the earth, and their armies, and the slaying of the remnant by the sword of him that sat upon the horse, foretell the overthrow and utter destruction of the allied armies of monarchy, by an enlightened confederated Republic in one great decisive battle.

The symbols are so numerous, the imagery so perfectly descriptive of each respective scene, and the correspondence of each member so wonderfully adapted to complete the symmetry of the whole, we are bound to behold their fulfillment in the rise and growing grandeur of a great consolidated Republic on the one hand, and the reconstruction of the autocracy of antiquity in some vast empire on the other. These two colossal powers will meet in a last decisive struggle.

So far as the historic panorama has disclosed the subject, the accumulating coincidences are remarkably true, and on a sublime scale. These two great powers are the United States of America and the monarchy of Russia, both extending the magnitude of their greatness; so that, in the present state of affairs, a perfect coincidence of facts answers a perfect description of prophecy. We look to the future for the finale of these startling wonders, to be fulfilled in a conflict that will enlist all nations, stir the world with commotion, and drench the earth with blood.

We now call your attention to a literal and most graphic description of the last conflict.

Ezekiel the priest, the son of Buzi, while amongst the captives by the river Chebor, saw the heavens open, and had visions of God.

In the thirty-eighth and thirty-ninth chapters of his prophecy, he gives us a full, literal, and detailed description of this battle; yet it is most astonishing that although this account is plain, presenting in the concrete and the minutiae the whole subject, commentators in the old continent declare that it is the most mysterious and perplexing portion of all Ezekiel's writings. Did it not appear uncharitable, we would be led to suppose that the only difficulty in the case was the doom of monarchy, so plainly announced, that a legitimate comment of its true meaning might not be favorably received by the fawning friends of the political systems of the old world. But God *"has magnified his word above all his name,"*

"And what his mouth in truth hath said,
His own almighty hand will do."

The invading army, and the multitudinous hosts of its allies, are particularly mentioned by their appropriate names and the countries they represent; the geographical location and territorial description of the land to be invaded; the character of its inhabitants, their quietude and prosperity; the unprovoked nature of the attack; the suicidal policy of the invasion, as declared by the Almighty; the solicitude of the invaded people to know the cause of the campaign; the universal agitation and commotion of the whole people so invaded; the battlefield; the Divine interposition in behalf of the invaded; the unbroken unanimity of all the States and Territories in resisting the foe; the overwhelming triumph over monarchy; the immensity of the armament, as seen in the sepulture of the slain and the wrecks of battle; the simultaneous insurrection of the subjects of monarchy at home; the glorious results of the contest: the annihilation of despotism, and the world wide extension of popular freedom – all, all are announced in the programme of the prophet.

First, then, let us **know who leads this invasion?**

"Son of man, set thy face against Gog, the land of Magog, the chief prince of Meshech and Tubal, and prophesy against him, and say, Thus saith the Lord God: Behold, I am against thee, O Gog, the chief prince of Meshech and Tubal: and I will turn thee back, and put hooks into thy jaws, and I will bring thee forth, and all thine army, horses and horsemen, all of them clothed with all sorts of armour, even a great company with bucklers and shields, all of them handling swords: Persia, Ethiopia, and Libya with them; all of them with shield and helmet: Gomer, and all his bands, the house of Togarmah of the north quarters, and all his bands: and many people with thee."

Now, whosoever these people may be, "the chief prince," or great leading sovereignty of the invasion is found among them. Hence this direct address of the Almighty to that prince. And that this prince is the headship of the alliance is evident from God's personal message to him: *"Be thou prepared, and prepare thyself, thou, and all thy company that are assembled unto thee, and be thou a guard unto them."* Here, then is the leading power marked out in the prophecy, to which the allied armies will be assembled.

This overwhelming power we shall demonstrate to be Russia.

The very names of the ancient patriarchs of the Russian dominions determine their location and nationality.

"Gog" signifies a prince or head of many countries.

"Magog, Gomer, Meshech, and Tubal," are four of the seven sons of Japheth (See Genesis 10; I Chronicles 1).

These patriarchs, according to Calmet, Brown, Bochart, and others, settled within the bounds of what is now the Russian dominions.

"Magog," says Josephus, "founded the Magogue, whom the Greeks call Sythee." Now, these Scythee are the Scythians who form almost one-fourth of Russian population. They extend from Hungary, Transylvania, and Wallachia, on the west, to the River Dan on the east. The Russian territory of this people embraces a large portion both of Europe and Asia.

"Meshech," the sixth son of Japheth, settled in the north-eastern portion of Asia Minor. His posterity extended from the shores of the Euxine Sea along to the south of Caucasus. He was the father of the Rossi and Moschi, who dispersed their colonies over a vast portion of Russian territory. And their names are preserved in the names of Russians and Moscovites to this day. The Septuagint version of the Old Testament renders the term Meshech by the words Mosch and Rosch; while Moscovy is a common name of Russia, and the city of Moscow is one of their principal cities.

"Tubal," or Tobal, the fifth son of Japheth, settled beyond the Caspian and Black Seas in the eastern possessions of Russia, embracing a very large portion of those dominions. The name of this patriarch is still preserved in the river Tobal, which waters an immense tract of Russian territory; and the city of Tobalski in Russia is still a monument to this son of Japheth.

From all which, it is certain that, as Magog, Meshech, and Tubal compose the present possessions of Russia, the sovereignty of that empire is the chief prince addressed in the prophetic message.

"Gomer, and all his bands; the house of Togarmah of the north quarters, and all his bands, and many people with thee."

"Gomer," another son of Japheth, settled farther down westward in Europe; and has left his name entailed in Hungary, in a city and country both known to this day as the city and country of Gomer.

"Togarmah," the son of Gomer, according to Cicero and Strabo, not only peopled a large portion of Western Europe, but sent settlements into Turcomania and Scythia in Russia.

Russia, then, according to the Scriptures, is the headship or leading power around which the multitudinous armies of allied monarchy shall be gathered together.

"Persia, Ethiopia, and Libya with them; all of them with shield and helmet."

Persia here represents the swarming hosts from the Asiatic possessions; Ethiopia and Libya, the armies of Africa.

"Thou shalt ascend and come like a storm, thou shalt be like a cloud to cover the land, thou, and all thy bands, and many people with thee."

The invasion is here announced by an armament such as the world never saw. For the millions that are to assemble under Gog or Russia embrace nearly all of Europe, as well as a large portion of Asia and Africa. This army is drafted from three continents to invade a fourth. It rises dismal as a cloud, and dreadful as a storm.

We must look to Russia, then, as the colossal giant of reconstructed monarchy, embodying the whole of autocracy in the last grand organization – embracing all the principles foreshadowed in the metallic symbol of the vision *"whose brightness was excellent, and the form thereof terrible."* In fact, the Emperor of all the Russians still bears the royal cognomen of the golden-headed monarchs of ancient Babylon. Who is the present Emperor of Russia? Alexander the **Czar**. And who are found among the monarchs of Assyria? Nobonazar, Nebuchadnezzar, and Belshazzar. These were not accidental terminations of their respective names, but were doubtless terms of Assyrian royalty. So also the Roman **Caesars**, which scarcely vary from the true pronunciation of the **czars**. We behold in Russia the original trunk of autocracy. In the time of Catharine, she arose in august magnitude, and entered into the European state system about the time of the rise of our great country. We see rising on the one hand and on the other, the two great powers that represent respectively their opposing principles of government that will come in collision in the last dreadful fray.

The United States of America, young and vigorous, arising in the Northern temperate zone, with untold resources, extending its borders from sea to sea, and from the lakes in the North to Heaven only knows how far South – she is the enlightened and uncompromising representative of popular freedom. And there is Russia in gigantic proportions, arising also in the Northern temperate zone, with her millions of warriors, now occupying one-seventh of earth's terra-firma, stretching from the Black Sea to the Arctic Ocean, and from the Baltic on the West, till her Cossacks almost hear the British drums beat in farther India. And she is the representative of absolutism.

These ascending powers, like two towering clouds culminating in the heavens, surcharged with electric ruin, will shock the world with their collision, and bathe the world in blood.

But allied with Russia will be the teeming myriads from all the empires on earth except France – belle France. France will be with us in the end, as she was with us in the beginning.* We feel warranted for this position.

(*In delivering the above sentence in the Hall of Representatives, the assembly turned their attention to a large life-like portrait of Lafayette, hanging on the walls of the Capitol, opposite that of Washington. We had not observed Lafayette's portrait till that moment, as it was on our left. The expression, "France will be with us in the end, as she was with us in the beginning," seemed to make profound sensation, as they saw no other nation on the canvas but France and America. The coincidence was impressive upon our own mind as it evidently was with the audience.)

Commentators agree, that when the state system in Europe is represented in the Apocalypse by the celestial bodies, France is appropriately denominated "the sun," not only from its vivacity and brilliancy, but especially from its central position to the rest of Europe. *"And I saw an angel standing in the sun; and he cried with a loud voice, saying to all the fowls that fly in the midst of heaven, Come, and gather yourselves together unto the supper of the great God, that ye may eat the flesh of kings,"* etc. (Revelation 19) This angel must, therefore, represent the genius of France, rejoicing over the downfall of monarchy; consequently, will be with America in the final struggle. A strong under-current for civil and religious liberty has frequently risen to the surface in the French nation; and under its power she will break her alliance with monarchy, and join the standard of liberty against the despotism of the world.

But England, true to her proud autocracy, will die for the Divine right of kings. Her policy will not be influenced by language, religion, nor blood; but in the final onset she will join the crusades against America.

When was she ever known to favor an oppressed people attempting to throw off the yoke of despotism? Look at her tender mercies toward her own children when struggling in the war for Independence. See how she let loose "the horrible hell-hounds of savage cruelty," when she turned the bloody Indian, with tomahawk and scalping-knife, upon helpless women and children; and even rewarded the savage furies with a pound sterling for every scalp that was taken, whether from the poor old man, the defenceless mother, or the sucking babe.

Look at her cruelties with her pagan slaves in India. Even now, who can look to China without emotion? Behold how she gloated over ill-fated Hungary. When the friends of freedom were immolated in crowds by Austrian despots – when delicate females were cowhided in the streets by the incarnate fiend Haynau – England, by a nod, could have suppressed the whole. Talk of English sympathy for the children of Africa in America! What consummate hypocrisy! When, at the same time, thousands of her own pauper people are suffered to live like beasts, or rather to die like dogs, if not confined for long years in her mines, without seeing the light of day, but working in traces like mules, on all-fours, to fatten the fortunes of English aristocracy. Do you doubt the picture? It is drawn by an official report to Parliament. Alas, let Ireland, from centuries of miserable oppression, say what heart has England to aid the friends of freedom against the despotisms of usurpation.

No: England will be allied with Russia. Her **policy, not her love**, may sustain amicable relations while it suits her, but no longer. But her glory is departing. She has gambled with the world till she has lost the sword. When the Empress of the British Isles visited the tomb of Napoleon, to pay honor to the ashes of the dead whom her own government had outlawed while living, it was then England's waning renown was seen in the rising splendors of the French nation. "Ichabod" is already written on the palaces of her power. Self-preservation will conglomerate the autocratic powers of the Old World in one stupendous attack upon that nation whose republican principles and brilliant example have already disquieted the repose of princes, and made each royal diadem a crown of thorns.

"Thus saith the Lord God: it shall also come to pass, that at the same time shall things come into thy mind, and thou shalt think an evil thought. Thou shalt say, I will go up to the land of unwalled villages: I will go to them that are at rest, that dwell safely, all of them dwelling without walls, and having neither bars nor gates. To take a spoil, and to take a prey; to turn thine hand upon the desolate places that are now inhabited, and upon the people that are gathered out of the nations, which have gotten cattle and goods, that dwell in the midst of the land." (Ezekiel 38) The Almighty pronounces the invasion impolitic – that the expedition was from *"an evil thought;"* and what was foreseen and foretold to be planned in weakness or wickedness, will, by its disastrous realization, confirm the truth of the Divine declaration.

The land to be invaded is, in the foregoing quotation, a literal and true description of the United States, and can apply to no other country or people under heaven. A country highly elevated – the land once a wilderness or desolate, but now inhabited – a *"land of unwalled villages"* . . . a *"people gathered out of the nations:"* – a people *"that dwell safely"* – proprietors of the country, dwelling at rest – a people prosperous in their fortunes, having *"gotten cattle and goods, dwelling in the midst of the land."* It is the same country described by the prophet *"between the two seas;"* and by Daniel, when, after describing the conquests of *"the willful king of the North,"* (Russia), in carrying his victorious armies *"into the glorious land,"* (Palestine), he hears tidings from the North and from the East which trouble him, and he *"comes in great wrath"* away from Palestine, and plants the tabernacles of his palaces *"in the glorious holy mountain."* Upon this high country he falls, and is *"broken without hands."* This glorious mountain cannot be Judea, for the invader has just returned from Judea to *"go up to the land of unwalled villages."*

"After many days thou shalt be visited: in the latter years thou shalt come unto the land that is gathered out of

many people . . . I will bring thee forth, and all thine army, horses and horsemen, all of them clothed with all sorts of armor, even a great company with bucklers and shields, all of them handling swords." Observe, the scene of this battle is laid *"in the latter years,"* which must correspond with the conflict which is yet to come; the expression being always understood in prophecy to refer to the thrilling times immediately preceding the millennium. The diversity of the implements of battle indicates the many nationalists enrolled for battle. Perhaps *"horses and horsemen"* peculiarly refer to the resources of Russia, who boasts that she can bring a million men into the field.

The battlefield – the Valley of the Mississippi: *"And it shall come to pass in that day, that I will give unto Gog a place there of graves in Israel, the valley of the passengers on the east of the sea."* (Ezekiel 39:11)

The philosophy of our language settles the location. When two things of the same class are spoken of in the same sentence, it is according to rhetoric, in referring to the greater of the two, simply to use the definite article "the." As the prophet had referred to both seas, the eastern and the great western, now it was proper simply to say *"the sea,"* that is, the Pacific, because it is the greater. This valley lies on the east of the Pacific, then, which is precisely the relative position of the Valley of the Mississippi. But this valley east of the Mississippi is *"the valley of passengers."*

How justly entitled to this appellation is our great Valley, more peculiarly so than any valley in the known world! See the thousands of vessels that convey tens of thousands of passengers on more than fifty thousand miles of the Father of Waters and its navigable tributaries! Look at the immense trains of people that daily traverse this valley in railroad cars, while caravan after caravan of emigrants are, and have been for years, pressing to the great West to dwell in all our vast new States and

Territories – and their number increases by swarming thousands! The Valley of the Mississippi, then, on the east of the sea, is *"the valley of passengers,"* and this is the battle-field of that last great conflict; for *"there,"* says God, *"will I give to Gog, and to the many people that are with them, a place of graves."* Joel lays the scene of this startling and sublime event also in a valley: *"Multitudes! Multitudes in the valley of decision!"*

The excitement and commotion amongst our own people will be overwhelming and universal. *"In that day there shall be a great shaking in the land of Israel, so that the fishes of the sea, and the fowls of heaven, and the beasts of the field, and all creeping things that creep upon the earth, shall shake at my presence, and the mountains shall be thrown down, and the steep places shall fall, and every wall shall fall to the ground."*

A time, indeed, of great consternation and trouble, such as has never been since the world began!

But firm and unbroken in the dreadful shock, our confederated Republic will remain an undivided unit. For, says God, *"I will call for a sword throughout all my mountains."* Every State and Territory will be in the field. Our glorious Union, then, from a Divine promise, shall never dissolve. No storm-cloud in the North, or volcanic eruption in the South, will ever divide our great country. Our noble vessel, with her live-oak timbers, will reel and quiver in the dreadful squall, but she will never founder! A child of Providence, born in the tempest and cradled in the storm, was early disciplined for the august destiny that awaits it:

> "A union of lakes, and a union of lands,
> A union no power shall sever;
> A union of hearts, and a union of hands,
> And the American Union for ever!"

In the darkness of that dreadful day, when the heavens are hung with the clouds of war, and the earth vibrates with the peals of battle; when the face of the valiant pale, and the heart of the brave is troubled; while storms portentous of annihilation howl around like the wailing of the damned – *"all these are but the beginning of sorrow:" "for there shall be great tribulation, such as was not since the beginning of the world to this time, no, nor ever shall be."*

It will be then, my countrymen, and not till then, that the heart of our great people will begin to understand the immediate presence of Almighty God, and the supervision of his providence in the rise, preservation, and destiny of our glorious Republic. *"So I will make my holy name known in the midst of my people Israel; and I will not let them pollute my holy name any more."* (Ezekiel 39)

In the universal calamity of those troublous times, we will be impelled to call upon Jehovah; and nothing can so effectually reveal the Divine presence and power as a whole nation looking to Heaven for help. To realize our dependence on Almighty God, and fully to know and appreciate the supervision of His hand, is doubtless one of the wise and gracious designs for the stormy ordeal through which we will pass. For in the very midnight of our troubles, Heaven will appear to our rescue. *"It shall come to pass at the same time, when Gog shall come against the land of Israel, saith the Lord God, that my fury shall come up in my face . . . I will put hooks in thy jaws, and turn thee back . . . I will call for a sword against him throughout all my mountains . . . And I will plead against him with pestilence and with blood; and I will rain upon him, and upon his bands, and upon the many people that are with him, an overflowing rain, and great hailstones, fire and brimstone.*

"Thus will I magnify myself, and sanctify myself; and I will be known in the eyes of many nations, and they shall know that I am the Lord . . . And I will smite thy bow out of thy left hand, and will cause thine arrows to fall out of thy right hand. Thou shalt fall upon the mountains of Israel, thou, and all thy bands, and the people that is with thee: I

will give thee unto the ravenous birds of every sort, and to the beasts of the field, to be devoured. Thou shalt fall upon the open field; for I have spoken it, saith the Lord God." (Ezekiel 39)

A similar description, with the same sublime imagery, of this battle of the great day of God Almighty will be found in the *Revelation* of John the evangelist. Both accounts close with the deep-toned period: *"Behold, it is done, saith the Lord God."* How immense that army! – doubtless many times greater than the forces with which Xerxes crossed the Hellespont into Greece; and he led two million six hundred thousand warriors, besides as many more sutlers and followers of the camp. How wide and dreadful the carnage! This we learn from the **seven months** occupied in burying the dead, for the victors were employed all that time in the rites of sepulture; and then the wreck of battle left implements enough to be used as fuel for seven years.

At the very time of the overthrow of Monarchy in the field, a revolutionary *"fire breaks out in the land of Magog"* and in the isles of the sea: the friends of freedom at home in Russia and Great Britain strike for liberty, and the work is done.

So closes the conflict of the world. Now paeans of gladness ring through the earth, while emancipated millions join the general joy. *"And I heard as it were the voice of a great multitude, and as the voice of many waters, and as the voice of mighty thunderings, saying, Alleluia: for the Lord God omnipotent reigneth."*

Henceforth, *"nations shall learn war no more."* Confederated Republics, under the counsel and example of the United States, will arise in the former, *"habitations of dragons,"* and the *"deserts"* of cruelty *"shall rejoice and blossom as the rose."* And, like an elder brother, our Republic will kindly instruct them in the principles of popular freedom. Now dawns the glorious day so often referred to in the Holy Scriptures – the millennium morning. Talk of converting the nations of the earth to God while monarchy lasts! What a mistake! Never can the Prince of Peace hold universal sway upon earth until the last vestige of earthly royalty is destroyed for ever.

But after the casting down of the thrones, the smiting of the great image, the taking of the beast and the false prophet, the reaping of the vintage and harvest of the earth, the overthrow of the dragon and his armies, the fall of the willful king, and the slaughter of the armies of God at the battle of the great day of God Almighty, that bright day shall begin, long the theme of so many promises to the good and true of every age, the hallowed hope of the Christian Church, and the song that made Judah's sacred mountains shake with joy. The cloudless splendor from *"a new heaven"* will beam upon the inhabitants of a *"a new earth"* in that happy millennium – a thousand years – when there will be but one kind of civil government known, and that will be Republicanism, and but one religion known, and that will be Christianity.

Not that every man will be a holy man, for the final judgment will come when wise and foolish virgins, the righteous and the wicked, will both be upon earth; but a long circle of ages called the millennium – a certain term given for an indefinite number of years – in which the means for the elevation of the world will be multiplied: commerce and trade, agriculture and manufactures, science and art, will extend, the gospel of the Son of God have universal welcome among the nations of the earth, and *"nations learn war no more."* Then will the apocalyptic angel, having the everlasting gospel to preach to every nation and people and tongue, sweep the breadth of heaven, and as his silvery pinions of light shave the level horizon, every island and continent shall bow obsequious to his message: *"Fear God, and give glory to him; and worship him that made heaven and earth, and the sea, and the fountains of waters."*

Then shall righteousness and peace among the nations walk, Messiah reign,

"And earth keep jubilee a thousand years."

George Washington
1732-1799
President from April 30, 1789 until March 4, 1797

George Washington's Vision
And Prophecy
For The United States of America

by John Grady, M.D.

The great British statesman and four times Prime Minister, William E. Gladstone, once proposed the creation of a grouping of pedestals for statues of history's most famous men. One pedestal stood higher than all the rest, and Gladstone was asked to identify the figure to be given the place of honor. Without a moment's hesitation, he named George Washington.

At the Continental Congress, meeting in Philadelphia, December 1799, one of Washington's finest military commanders, the famous cavalry general, Henry "Light-Horse Harry" Lee, then Congressman from Virginia (and later to become that state's governor), upon hearing of the death of our first president, rose to his feet and with tears in his eyes spoke for all Americans for all time when he said to Washington, "First in war, first in peace, and first in the hearts of his countrymen."

Many students of history consider George Washington to be the greatest man who ever lived. Certainly, he was the greatest American – a brilliant, educated, successful man who risked everything for the freedom of our country.

Washington was a man of great moral character. He was forthright, honest, charitable and a gentle man of quiet modesty and proper deportment – considerate, kind and courteous.

Washington was also a man of great talent. He was knowledgeable in agriculture, was a surveyor with an established reputation, and early in life became a land owner of some importance and considerable wealth.

He was held in such respect that at the age of 21 he was made a Major and Adjutant of the Virginia Militia, and so distinguished himself that at the age of 23 he was made Commander-in-Chief of the Frontier Forces of Virginia.

Washington had a commanding appearance. He was the most physically impressive of all of our Presidents, and in his prime stood over 6 feet 4 inches tall and was a lean and powerful 225 pounds. In addition, this handsome figure had a distinct military bearing.

Washington was appropriately described by colleagues and writers of the time as ". . . straight, tall, wide-shouldered, with head well shaped, large straight nose, penetrating blue-gray eyes, a long handsome face terminating in a good firm chin, clear fair skin, firm mouth, and a commanding countenance, with speech, movement and gestures which are agreeable, differential, engaging and graceful."

Most important of all, Washington was a man with a total sense of responsibility, unquestioned integrity and deep devotion to God.

Among the many outstanding men of leadership in the American Colonies, Washington stood out above all. Once the War for Independence began, he was quickly and logically chosen Commander-in-Chief of the Colonial Forces. Washington had the impossible task of taking a few thousand untrained volunteers and leading them against the armies of the world's greatest empire. Great Britain was a powerful and progressive nation with colonies and influence around the world, and she had mighty armies and fleets to defend her possessions. England could accurately boast that the sun never set upon her flag or the British Empire.

To add to the difficulties was the fact that the American Colonies were not united, were economically weak, had no standing army and no navy, and had only three million people, who were seriously divided as to whether or not to fight for freedom.

It is not known what percentage of the Colonists genuinely supported the cause for freedom. Many of those who opposed independence constantly gave help, comfort and support to the enemy. Probably no more than 3% of the people in the Colonies actually took part in the fight for American independence. Then, as now, apathy, self-interests, uncertainty and fear prevailed among a large portion of the population.

Once the Declaration of Independence had been signed and Washington's forces were pitted against the British, his army was so greatly outnumbered and so ill equipped that many thought him foolhardy to even attempt to fight the most powerful nation in the world. Seldom in all of history has such a task been undertaken under such unfavorable conditions. However, Patrick Henry in his famous "Give me liberty or give me death" speech hit directly upon his reasons for hoping for ultimate victory when he said, "God will raise up friends to fight our battles for us."

General Washington led his men with a passion, courage and fortitude that could come only from total dedication. When the Continental Congress did not, or could not, send the funds for his soldiers' supplies and salaries, Washington paid for them out of his own pocket. He gained and held the allegiance of his men because he was fair, firm, resolute and dedicated. Moreover, he was a devoutly Christian man who made no apology for prayer. He repeatedly called upon God for deliverance and victory in the struggle for freedom.

The cover paintings of George Washington kneeling in prayer in the snow-covered woods of Valley Forge are based on fact. He believed that God would lead him to victory, and anyone who has read his handwritten letters and documents cannot help but be impressed by his reliance on the Almighty and his deep belief in Divine Guidance.

Strengthened by a sense of duty and honor, driven by a love of freedom and a hunger for justice, sustained by faith and confidence in Divine Providence, George Washington would not fail. He would fulfill his destiny. This uncommon man would lead the colonial forces to victory, become the father of our country, be unanimously acclaimed our first President, and set the course for what was to become history's greatest nation.

Little wonder then that he was shown great favor by the God of our universe. As the prophets of old were shown the destiny of mankind, so was Washington shown the destiny of our nation. General Washington had an unusual and profound spiritual experience in Valley Forge. He was given a vision of such momentous importance that it prompts the writing of this paper and the dissemination of this information to all concerned Americans.

Washington told of the event shortly after it took place. It was repeated to his close confidantes and fellow patriots during the 22 years he lived after its occurrence. And it has been carried in print from time to time over the past 200 years. However, since spiritual experiences tend to be ignored by secular historians, it has remained at times an obscurity.

Thomas Jefferson best expressed the relationship between man's highest aspiration and the great Creator when he wrote, "God who gave us life, gave us liberty." Throughout history, as is well documented in Holy Scripture and readily attested to by millions of observant people, God has raised up individuals, usually temporal leaders, to fulfill the destiny of men and nations.

It is the personal opinion of this writer that God moulded, inspired and directed George Washington. He was, indeed, chosen to be a special man, at a special time, for a special purpose.

Various accounts of George Washington's vision and prophecy all agree in content. There have been only minor variations in some details as the story was repeated over the years by those to whom it was related by General Washington.

The place was Valley Forge in the cold and bitter winter of 1777. Washington's army had suffered several reverses and the situation was desperate. Food was scarce. The Continental Congress was not sending supplies or money. Some of the troops did not even have shoes to wear in the snow. Many soldiers were sick and dying from disease and exposure. Morale was at an all-time low, and there was great agitation in the Colonies against the continued effort to secure our freedom from England. Nevertheless, General Washington was determined to see the struggle through.

These are the words of a first-hand observer, Anthony Sherman, who was there and describes the situation: "You doubtless heard the story of Washington's going to the thicket to pray. Well, it is not only true, but he used often to pray in secret for aid and comfort from God, the interposition of whose Divine Providence brought us safely through the darkest days of tribulation.

"One day, I remember it well, when the chilly winds whistled through the leafless trees, though the sky was cloudless and the sun shown brightly, he remained in his quarters nearly all the afternoon alone. When he came out, I noticed that his face was a shade paler than usual. There seemed to be something on his mind of more than ordinary importance. Returning just after dusk, he dispatched an orderly to the quarters who was presently in attendance. After a preliminary conversation of about an hour,

Washington, gazing upon his companion with that strange look of dignity which he alone commanded, related the event that occurred that day.

"This afternoon, as I was sitting at this table engaged in preparing a dispatch, something seemed to disturb me. Looking up, I beheld standing opposite me a singularly beautiful female. So astonished was I, for I had given strict orders not to be disturbed, that it was some moments before I found language to inquire the cause of her presence. A second, a third and even a fourth time did I repeat my question, but received no answer from my mysterious visitor except a slight raising of her eyes.

"By this time I felt strange sensations spreading through me. I would have risen but the riveted gaze of the being before me rendered volition impossible. I assayed once more to address her, but my tongue had become useless, as though it had become paralyzed.

"A new influence, mysterious, potent, irresistible, took possession of me. All I could do was to gaze steadily, vacantly at my unknown visitor. Gradually the surrounding atmosphere seemed as if it had become filled with sensations, and luminous. Everything about me seemed to rarify, the mysterious visitor herself becoming more airy and yet more distinct to my sight than before. I now began to feel as one dying, or rather to experience the sensations which I have sometimes imagined accompany dissolution. I did not think, I did not reason, I did not move; all were alike impossible. I was only conscious of gazing fixedly, vacantly at my companion.

"Presently I heard a voice saying, 'Son of the Republic, look and learn,' while at the same time my visitor extended her arm eastwardly. I now beheld a heavy white vapor at some distance rising fold upon fold. This gradually dissipated, and I looked upon a strange scene. Before me lay spread out in one vast plain all the countries of the world – Europe, Asia, Africa and America. I saw rolling and tossing between Europe and America the billows of the Atlantic, and between Asia and America lay the Pacific.

"'Son of the Republic,' said the same mysterious voice as before, 'look and learn.' At that moment I beheld a dark, shadowy being, like an angel, standing, or rather floating, in mid-air between Europe and America. Dipping water out of the ocean in the hollow of each hand, he sprinkled some upon America with his right hand, while with his left hand he cast some on Europe. Immediately a cloud raised from these countries, and joined in mid-ocean. For a while it remained stationary, and then moved slowly westward until it enveloped America in its murky folds. Sharp flashes of lightning gleamed through it at intervals, and I heard the smothered groans and cries of the American people.

"A second time the angel dipped water from the ocean, and sprinkled it out as before. The dark cloud was then drawn back to the ocean, in whose heaving billows it sank from view. A third time I heard the mysterious voice saying, 'Son of the Republic, look and learn.' I cast my eyes upon America and beheld villages and towns and cities springing up one after another until the whole land from the Atlantic to the Pacific was dotted with them.

"Again, I heard the mysterious voice say, 'Son of the Republic, the end of the century cometh, look and learn.' At this the dark shadowy angel turned his face southward, and from Africa I saw an ill-omened spectre approach our land. It flitted slowly over every town and city of the latter. The inhabitants presently set themselves in battle array against each other. As I continued looking I saw a bright angel upon whose brow rested a crown of light, on which was traced the word 'Union,' bearing the American flag which he placed between the divided nation, and said, 'Remember ye are brethren.' Instantly, the inhabitants, casting from them their weapons, became friends once more, and united around the National Standard.

"And again I heard the mysterious voice saying; 'Son of the Republic, look and learn.' At this the dark shadowy angel placed a trumpet to his mouth, and blew three distinct blasts; and taking water from the ocean, he sprinkled it upon Europe, Asia and Africa. Then my eyes beheld a fearful scene: from each of these countries arose thick, black clouds that were soon joined into one. Throughout this mass there gleamed a dark red light by which I saw hordes of armed men, who, moving with the cloud, marched by land and sailed by sea to America. Our country was enveloped in this volume of cloud, and I saw these vast armies devastate the whole country and burn the villages, towns and cities that I beheld springing up. As my ears listened to the thundering of the cannon, clashing of swords, and the shouts and cries of millions in mortal combat, I heard again the mysterious voice saying, 'Son of the Republic, look and learn.' When the voice had ceased, the dark shadowy angel placed his trumpet once more to his mouth, and blew a long and fearful blast.

"Instantly a light as of a thousand suns shown down from above me, and pierced and broke into fragments the dark cloud which enveloped America. At the same moment the angel upon whose head still shone the word Union, and who bore our national flag in one hand and a sword in the other, descended from the heavens attended by legions of white spirits. These immediately joined the inhabitants of America, who I perceived were well nigh overcome, but who, immediately taking courage again, closed up their broken ranks and renewed the battle.

"Again, amid the fearful noise of the conflict, I heard the mysterious voice say, 'Son of the Republic, look and learn.' As the voice ceased, the shadowy angel for the last time dipped water from the ocean and sprinkled it upon America. Instantly the dark cloud rolled back, together with the armies it had brought, leaving the inhabitants of the land victorious!

"Then once more I beheld the villages, towns and cities springing up where I had seen them before, while the bright angel, planting the azure standard he had brought in the midst of them, cried with a loud voice: 'While the stars remain, and the heavens send down dew upon the earth, so long shall the Union last.' And taking from his brow the crown on which was blazoned the word 'Union,' he placed it upon the Standard, while the people, kneeling down, said, 'Amen.'

"The scene instantly began to fade and dissolve, and I at last saw nothing but the rising, curling vapor I at first beheld. This also disappearing, I found myself once more gazing upon the mysterious visitor, who, in the same voice I had heard before, said, 'Son of the Republic, what you have seen is thus interpreted: Three great perils will come upon the Republic. The most fearful is the third, but in this greatest conflict the whole world united shall not prevail against her. Let every child of the Republic learn to live for his God, his land and the Union.' With these words the vision vanished, and I started from my seat and felt that I had seen a vision wherein had been shown to me the birth, progress, and destiny of the United States."

Thus ended General George Washington's vision and prophecy for the United States of America as told in his own words.

Quotes from Our Forefathers

Christopher Columbus
(name meaning *Christ-bearer*)
(1451-1506) Explorer and Navigator

In his *Libro de las Profecias* (Book of Prophecies*)*, Columbus wrote:

*"For the execution of the journey to the Indies I did not make use of intelligence, mathematics or maps. It is simply the **fulfillment of what Isaiah had prophesied**. All this is what I desire to write down for you in this book."*

The following are two of the many excerpts from Isaiah that he quoted in his book: *"Surely the isles* [undeveloped lands] *wait for me, and the ships of Tarshish* [Spain] *first, to bring thy sons from far, their silver and their gold with them, unto the name of the Lord thy God, and to the Holy One of Israel, because he hath glorified thee."* (Isaiah 60:9) *"I will also give thee* [Israel] *for a light to the Gentiles, that thou mayest be my salvation unto the end of the earth."* (Isaiah 49:6)

Sir Francis Drake (1540-1596)
English Navigator

He was one of the first explorers to sail around the world. In his letter to John Foxe, author of *Foxe's Book of Martyrs*, he wrote: ". . . *God may be glorified, His church, our Queen and country preserved, the enemies of truth vanquished, that we might have continual peace in **Israel**. Our enemies are many, **but our Protector commandeth the whole earth**."*

John Robinson (1576-1625)
English Congregationalist Preacher

He was one of the pastors who left with the Pilgrims to go to America. *He believed that God had called His people to go to this land to build a **new Jerusalem**.* He also said "the people of God in old times were called out of Babylon civil, the place of their bodily bondage, and were to come to Jerusalem, and there to build the Lord's Temple . . . so are the people of God now to go out of Babylon spiritual to Jerusalem and to build themselves as lively stones into a spiritual house, or temple, for the Lord to dwell in..."

Pilgrim and Puritan Testimony

Many Pilgrims and Puritans upon coming to America called themselves *"The Seed of Abraham," "God's Servants," "His Chosen,"* and *"A Vine Out of Egypt into the Wilderness."* They also called this land *"The Wilderness," "New Canaan Land,"* and *"The New Promised Land."* They built our nation upon the Laws of God and the teachings of Christ, and the United States of America became the greatest nation in history.

John Cotton (1584-1652)
Puritan Preacher

In his farewell sermon to his congregation in England, he stated that God had selected them as His ***new chosen people*** to come to the virgin wilderness of the American continent, which had been reserved for them all these years. He stated they were the new Israelites, and quoted the promise of God to His people found in II Samuel 7:10. *"I will appoint a place for my people Israel, and will plant them, that they may dwell in a place of their own."*

John Winthrop (1588-1649)
Founder and First Governor of the
Massachusetts Bay Colony
(spoken on board the Arabella in 1630)

"We shall find that the **God of Israel is among us**, when ten of us shall be able to resist a thousand of our enemies, when He shall make us a praise and glory, that men of succeeding plantations shall say, 'The Lord make it like that of New England.' For we must consider that **we shall be as a City upon a Hill, the eyes of all people are upon us**."

Cotton Mather (1663-1728)
Colonial Clergyman

"In our hastening voyage unto the history of a **new-English Israel**...These good people were now satisfied, that had as plain a command of heaven to attempt a removal, as ever **their father Abraham** had for his leaving the Chaldean territories...Among these passengers were divers worthy and useful men, who were come to seek the welfare of this **little Israel**...to give them such hearts as were in Abraham, and others of their famous and faithful fathers... an introduction unto this piece of New-English history; that when some ecclesiastical oppressions drive a **colony of the truest Israelites** into the remoter parts of the world, there was an academy quickly founded in that colony..."

Samuel Adams (1722-1803)
(In a speech to the signers
of the Declaration of Independence, August 1, 1776)

"Looking for **God's Kingdom on this continent**, we have this day restored the Sovereign, to Whom alone men ought to be obedient. He reigns in heaven and...from the rising to the setting sun, may **His Kingdom come**."

Ezra Stiles (1727-1795)
(May 8, 1783 sermon commemorating the anniversary
of his appointment as President of Yale College)

"Already does the new constellation of the United States begin to realize this glory. It has already risen to an acknowledged sovereignty among the republics and kingdoms of the world. And we have reason to hope, and, I believe, to expect, that God has still greater blessings in store for **this vine** which his own right hand hath planted.

"...Our degree of population is such as to give us reason to expect that this will become a great people...This will be a great, a very great nation... Should this prove a future fact, how applicable would be the text, 'when the LORD shall have made his **American-Israel** high above all nations which he has made,' in numbers, and in praise, and in name, and in honour!

"...And thus the American Republic, by illuminating the world with truth and liberty, would be exalted and made high among the nations, in praise, and in name, and in honour. I doubt not this is the honour reserved for us."

"...The United States are under peculiar obligations to become a holy people unto the LORD our God..."

"...And who can tell how extensive a blessing this **American Joseph** may become to the whole human race, although once despised by his brethren, exiled, and sold into Egypt?"

Jonas Clark (1730-1805)
New England Clergyman

On the night that Paul Revere arrived at Mr. Clark's house to warn of the approaching British troops, he was asked by his guests, John Hancock and Samuel Adams, if the people would fight. He replied that he had "trained them for this very hour; they would fight, and, if need be, die, too, under the shadow of the house of God." The next day, April 19, 1775, upon seeing the first blood of the Revolution shed near his house, he said: *"From this day will be dated the liberty of the world."*

"Under this happy constitution we have seen, to universal satisfaction, that blessed prophecy concerning God's people after their return from captivity, **literally fulfilled unto us**: *'...and their congregation shall be established before me... And their nobles shall be of themselves, and their governor shall proceed from the midst of them'..."* (Jer. 30:20-21)

George Washington (1732-1799)
First President of the United States

"It is impossible to rightly govern the world without God and the Bible. It is impossible to account for the creation of the universe without the agency of a Supreme Being. It is impossible to govern the universe without the aid of a Supreme Being. It is impossible to reason without arriving at a Supreme Being."

John Adams (1735-1826)
Second President of the United States

"We have no government armed with power capable of contending with human passions unbridled by morality and religion. Avarice, ambition, revenge, or gallantry, would break the strongest cords of our Constitution as a whale goes through a net. **Our Constitution was made only for a moral and religious people. It is wholly inadequate to the government of any other.**" – October 11, 1798

Patrick Henry (1736-1799)
American Revolutionary Leader and Orator
(1765 Speech to the House of Burgesses)

"It cannot be emphasized too clearly and too often that **this nation was founded, not by religionists, but by Christians; not on religion, but on the gospel of Jesus Christ**. For this very reason, peoples of other faiths have been afforded asylum, prosperity, and freedom of worship here."

Charles Carroll (1737-1832)
(Signer of the Declaration of Independence)

"**Without morals a republic cannot subsist any length of time**; they therefore who are decrying the Christian religion, whose morality is so sublime and pure...are undermining the solid foundation of morals, the best security for the duration of free governments."

Thomas Paine (1737-1809)
Author of *Common Sense*

"It has been the error of the schools to teach astronomy, and all the other sciences, and subjects of natural philosophy, as accomplishments only; whereas they should be taught theologically, or with reference to the Being who is the author of them: **for all the principles of science are of divine origin. Man cannot make, or invent, or contrive principles: he can only discover them; and he ought to look through the discovery to the Author.**"

"The evil that has resulted from the error of the schools, in teaching natural philosophy as an accomplishment only, has been that of generating in the pupils a species of atheism. Instead of looking through the works of creation to the Creator Himself, they stop short, and employ the knowledge they acquire to create doubts of His existence. They labour with studied ingenuity to ascribe every thing they behold to innate properties of matter, and jump over all the rest by saying, that matter is eternal." "The Existence of God – 1810"

Thomas Jefferson (1743-1826)
Third President of the United States

He was one of the founders of our nation and author of the Declaration of Independence. In a letter to Dr. Walter Jones in 1814, remembering the death of George Washington, he wrote: *"I felt on his death, with my countrymen, that verily a great man hath fallen this day in Israel."* He stated in his Second Inaugural Address: *"I shall need, too, the favor of that Being in whose hands we are, who led our fathers as Israel of old, from their native land and planted them in a country flowing with the necessities and comforts of life."* Jefferson's idea for the great seal of the United States was Moses leading the children of **Israel** through the wilderness with the pillars of fire and clouds.

(Excerpts inscribed on the walls of the Jefferson Memorial)

"God who gave us life gave us liberty. And can the liberties of a nation be thought secure when we have removed their only firm basis, a conviction in the minds of the people that these liberties are a gift from God? That they are not to be violated but with His wrath? Indeed I tremble for my country when I reflect that God is just, and that His justice cannot sleep forever."

The Boston Tea Party (1773)
(The men of Marlborough, Massachusetts)

"A free-born people are not required by the religion of Jesus Christ to submit to tyranny, but may make use of such power as God has given them to recover and support their laws and liberties ... [We] implore the Ruler above the skies, that he would make bare His arm in defense of His Church and people, and let **Israel** go."

Benjamin Rush (1745-1813)
Founding Father

"I lament that we waste so much time and money in punishing crimes and take so little pains to prevent them – we neglect the only means of establishing and perpetuating our republican forms of government; that is, the universal education of our youth in the principles of Christianity by means of the Bible; for this Divine Book, above all others, constitutes the soul of republicanism." "By withholding the knowledge of [the Scriptures] from children, we deprive ourselves of the best means of awakening moral sensibility in their minds." [Letter written (1790's) in Defense of the Bible in all schools in America]

"Christianity is the only true and perfect religion."

"If moral precepts alone could have reformed mankind, the mission of the Son of God into our world would have been unnecessary."

James Madison (1751-1836)
Fourth President of the United States

At the Constitutional Convention of 1787, James Madison proposed the plan to divide the central government into three branches. He discovered this model of government from the Perfect Governor, as he read Isaiah 33:22, *"For the LORD is our judge* [Judicial], *the LORD is our lawgiver* [Legislative], *the LORD is our king* [Executive]*; He will save us."*

Noah Webster (1758-1843)
Author of Webster's Dictionary

"Let it be impressed on your mind that God commands you to choose for rulers just men who will rule in the fear of God [Exodus 18:21]. . . . If the citizens neglect their duty and place unprincipled men in office, the government will soon be corrupted . . . . If our government fails to secure public prosperity and happiness, it must be because the citizens neglect the Divine commands, and elect bad men to make and administer the laws."

"The moral principles and precepts contained in the Scriptures ought to form the basis of all our civil constitutions and laws. All the miseries and evils which men suffer from vice, crime, ambition, injustice, oppression, slavery, and war, proceed from their despising or neglecting the precepts contained in the Bible."

Jedediah Morse (1761-1826)
United States Clergyman and Geographer

"To the kindly influence of Christianity we owe that degree of civil freedom, and political and social happiness which mankind now enjoys . . . . **Whenever the pillars of Christianity shall be overthrown, our present republican forms of government, and all blessings which flow from them, must fall with them."**

John Quincy Adams (1767-1848)
Sixth President of the United States

"Nowhere in history is God's hand more evident than in the establishment of America."

"Is it not that the Declaration of Independence first organized the social compact on the foundation of the Redeemer's mission upon earth?

"That it laid the cornerstone of human government upon the first precepts of Christianity and gave to the world the first irrevocable pledge of the **fulfillment of the prophecies** announced directly from Heaven at the birth of the Saviour and **predicted** by the greatest of the Hebrew prophets 600 years before."

Andrew Jackson (1767-1845)
Seventh President of the United States

"You have the highest of human trusts dedicated to your care. Providence has showered on this favored land blessings without number, and has chosen you as the guardians of freedom, to preserve it for the benefit of the human race. May He who holds in His hands the destiny of nations make you worthy of the favors He has bestowed, and enable you, with pure hearts and hands and sleepless vigilance, to guard and defend to the end of time the great charge He has committed to your keeping."

Abied Abbott
(In a Thanksgiving sermon, 1799)

"It has often been remarked that our people of the United States come nearer to a parallel with Ancient Israel than any other nation upon the globe. Hence our **American Israel** is a term frequently used; and common consent allows it apt and proper."

Abraham Lincoln (1809-1865)
Sixteenth President of the United States
(proclamation during National Day of Fasting and Prayer,
April 30, 1863)

"It is the duty of nations, as well as of men, to owe their dependence upon the overruling power of God . . . and to recognize the sublime truth, announced in the holy scriptures and proven by all history, **that those nations only are blessed whose God is the LORD**...

"We have been the recipients of the choicest bounties of heaven. We have been preserved, these many years, in peace and prosperity. We have grown in numbers, wealth and power, as no other nation has ever grown. But we have forgotten God! We have forgotten the gracious hand which has preserved us in peace, and multiplied and enriched and strengthened us; and we have vainly imagined, in the deceitfulness of our hearts, that all these blessings were produced by some superior wisdom and virtue of our own."

(John) Calvin Coolidge (1872-1933)
Thirtieth President of the United States

"They [Puritan forefathers] were an inspired body of men. It has been said *that God sifted the nations that He might send choice grain into the wilderness...* Who can fail to see in it the hand of destiny? Who can doubt that it has been guided by a Divine Providence"?

Ronald Reagan (1911-2004)
Fortieth President of the United States

"You and I have a rendezvous with destiny. We will preserve for our children this, the last best hope of man on earth ..."

Lest we forget...

Turn, O backsliding children, saith the Lord; for I am married unto you: and I will take you one of a city, and two of a family, and I will bring you to Zion:

And I will give you pastors according to mine heart, which shall feed you with knowledge and understanding.

And it shall come to pass, when ye be multiplied and increased in the land, in those days, saith the Lord, they shall say no more, The ark of the covenant of the Lord: neither shall it come to mind: neither shall they remember it; neither shall they visit it; neither shall that be done any more. – Jeremiah 3:14-16